Day by Day These Things We Pray

UNCOVERING ANCIENT RHYTHMS OF PRAYER

ARTHUR BOERS

Herald Press

Waterloo, Ontario
Scottdale, Pennsylvania

Library and Archives Canada Cataloguing in Publication
Boers, Arthur Paul, 1957-
  Day by day, these things we pray : uncovering ancient
rhythms of prayer / Arthur Paul Boers.

Originally publ.: Brewster, Mass. : Paraclete Press, c2003,
  under title: The rhythm of God's grace.
"This is a revision and expansion of an earlier volume, The
  rhythm of God's grace ...".—Introd.
ISBN 978-0-8361-9530-9
  1. Prayer—Christianity. 2. Spiritual life—Christianity. I. Title.

BV199.D3B643 2010   248.3'2   C2010-905179-3

DAY BY DAY THESE THINGS WE PRAY
Copyright © 2010 by Herald Press, Scottdale, PA 15683
  Released simultaneously in Canada by Herald Press,
  Waterloo, Ont. N2L 6H7. All rights reserved
Library of Congress Control Number: 2010933403
Canadiana Entry Number: C2010-905179-3
International Standard Book Number: 978-0-8361-9530-9
Printed in the United States of America
Cover by Reuben Graham

15 14 13 12 11 10   10 9 8 7 6 5 4 3 2 1

To order or request information please call 1-800-245-7894
or visit www.heraldpress.com.

Dedicated with joy, appreciation,
and deep gratitude to our children,
Erin Margaret
and
Paul Edward.

"Children are a heritage from the Lord,
and the fruit of the womb is a gift."
—Psalm 127:4, Book of Common Prayer

Contents

Foreword

One could predict that it would only be a matter of time before someone would rediscover the ancient rhythm of daily prayer. That someone is Arthur Boers. His work is not only a pioneer work among Protestants, but also a much needed primer for the whole church.

Speaking to our need, to the contemporary church's need to reapproach early church rhythms of prayer, Boers writes: "We can only know God's presence at all times if we set aside certain times for prayer." This is the sentence that jumped out at me, speaking clearly the key to the whole passion and burden of this book.

Fixed times of prayer, as the church has attested to throughout history, is in no way binding or legalistic. If anything, fixed times of prayer release our lives into the freedom of unceasing prayer!

But for many, and historically, this form of prayer has been lost. Though, and it has been interesting to watch, a warm change has come to worship and prayer for Protestants since the early seventies.

Why? It began with the liturgical church, simply, the trickle-down effect of a document of Vatican II titled "The Impact of the Constitution on the Sacred Liturgy." This document encouraged the return to liturgical prayer, to fixed times of prayer. Word quickly spread within the liturgical churches. And by the late seventies and eighties, prayer books were developed within these liturgical churches to reflect a return to early church forms of prayer. A true sense of commonality, togetherness, and ecumenism in prayer emerged and grew.

The impact among Protestants was slower moving. Yet a thirst for returning to the roots of the early church resulted, growing toward the inevitable conclusion: There is more to the church than its Protestant history. Our common roots go deeper, and there is something we share with the liturgical churches. The quest for deepening roots has led some in the Protestant tradition to look toward the early and medieval church. The result? Many Protestants from the Free Church tradition have sought to recover the church's heritage in worship, prayer, and spirituality.

Attending to this desire for deep historical roots in prayer, Arthur Paul Boers has given us a book that introduces us to liturgical prayer, to its history, and to ways to begin discovering our own journeys of prayer.

I welcome this work and the sensitivity Dr. Boers shows to teaching daily prayer to those who know little about this great Christian devotion of the early church. The clarity, the profundity, and the challenge of *Day by Day These Things We Pray* will be of great help to all of us who seek to be more deeply aware of the intimacy with God established in prayer.

—*Robert Webber (1933-2007)*
  Meyers Professor of Ministry
  Northern Baptist Seminary

Acknowledgments

Since this volume is a revision and expansion of an earlier book, *The Rhythm of God's Grace*,[1] the communion of sainted supporters keeps growing wider.

I offer hearty gratitude to Eleanor Kreider, Barb Nelson Gingerich, John Rempel, and Mary Schertz in their stellar work of editing, testing, and producing volumes of the prayer book *Take Our Moments and Our Days*.[2] Behind the scenes and along the way, extraordinary assistance was offered by James Nelson Gingerich, Gloria Jost, Marlene Kropf, Lois Siemens, Rebecca Slough, and Willard Swartley. It was a pleasure to work with such committed and creative colleagues; even now that I have moved some distance away, I continue to admire their achievements.

I also express appreciation to the late Paul Fretz and his wife, Viola, and their daughter, Bev. I value their tremendous support for my ministry, all the while serving as exemplars to me of Christian faithfulness.

It has been a pleasure to work closely with Herald Press once more, and I am indebted to Amy Gingerich, my high school buddy John Longhurst (how the years fly!), and Russ Eanes. And thanks too to Paraclete Press for making this all possible and for its support of *The Rhythm of God's Grace*.

Michael David Lysack first introduced me to common prayer (Taizé's *Praise in All Our Days*),[3] helping me to pray again when I was in grief.

In my decades of visits, St. Gregory's Abbey taught me more about prayer and worship than anyone else. I am grateful for the privilege of being an oblate there.

My last congregation, Bloomingdale Mennonite, gave me room and flexibility for sabbatical times, pilgrimages, writing, and above all, prayer. The Elders back then—Ray Boehm, Eleanor Snyder, and Myron Stevanus—supported my studies of fixed-hour prayer. Brave souls there joined my morning and evening prayer project, learning about and working hard at an unfamiliar discipline: Pauline Bauman, Viola Fretz, Twila Lebold, Lorna McDougall, Sandra Mooibroek, AnneMarie Smit, Pauline and Richard Weiland, and Linda Worth.

The Leadership Commission and Doris Gascho, the (former) Conference Minister of Mennonite Conference of Eastern Canada, granted sabbatical support.

Helen Kenik Mainelli (formerly at Northern Baptist Theological Seminary) was the single most important person in my Doctor of Ministry work on common prayer: consulting, encouraging, and supporting me from the beginning. Other key persons helping me there were Gerald Borchert and Robert Webber (who also gave invaluable publishing advice and encouragement). Peter Erb of Wilfrid Laurier University and Joyce Ann

Zimmerman of the Institute for Liturgical Ministry led me in comprehending and unpacking key historical and theological ideas underlying the liturgy of the hours.

The Louisville Institute (funded by the Lilly Endowment) made possible my journey to Europe to innovative ecumenical and internationally influential communities, my visits to extraordinary monasteries in North America, and my time spent writing this book. It is no exaggeration to say that it and its officers, Jim Lewis and David Wood, changed my life. The "Apart and Yet a Part" writers' retreat at the Collegeville Institute in 2010 was a hospitable and congenial setting for revising this volume. Special thanks are due to Donald Ottenhoff, executive director.

Various communities welcomed, inspired, and challenged me in Europe: David Adam and others at St. Mary the Virgin Church; Ray Simpson and the Community of Aidan and Hilda on Holy Isle; members, staff, and guests at Iona; Brothers Jean-Marie and Émile and their community of Taizé; and everyone at Northumbria. I was grateful for weeklong visits at the Monastery of Christ in the Desert (New Mexico) and St. John's Abbey (Minnesota).

My previous employer, Associated Mennonite Biblical Seminary, also encouraged me in my ministry of writing generally and specifically in promoting the practice of the divine hours for the church today. My present employer, Tyndale Seminary, also supports research and writing for the sustaining of Christian life, and I am thankful for what that makes possible.

I have appreciated the opportunity to test ideas in *Canadian Mennonite*, *Christian Century*, *Christianity Today*, the *Kitchener-Waterloo Record*, *CrossPoint*, *Reformed Worship*, and *The Mennonite*.

I am grateful to Biff Weidman and the Emmaus House community, who welcomed me to morning prayers (when I awoke on time) during a hard transition. Other Anabaptists who particularly encouraged this project include Hulitt Gloer, Nelson Kraybill, and Alan Kreider.

Encouragement and good counsel came from Dorothy Bass, Eugene Peterson, and Phyllis Tickle. (And thanks too for their writings.)

My daughter, Erin, gave invaluable assistance in transcribing interviews and checking references.

As always, the greatest thanks go to my wife, Lorna McDougall, and our children, Erin Margaret and Paul Edward, who are my three dearest friends and are graciously supportive of my work, studies, travels, research, and intense times of writing. Without them, not only would this work be impossible: it also would not be worthwhile.

I am blessed beyond words.

Introduction

People sometimes ask why I write, and my answer always depends on how much time there is for conversation. My parents often reminded me that as I left the house for my first day of kindergarten, I eagerly predicted: "Today I will learn to read and write!" I longed for both practices way back then and all the time ever since, too.

Writing is one of my deepest needs, perhaps even a compulsion, like reading, prayer, and friendship. When I go without it for too long, I get off balance, out of sorts, and cranky. I have known this for a long time about myself.

Yet writing not only was something individual for me. As a child and then teenager, I first wrote a lot that was for my eyes alone: a forgettable mystery novel when I was twelve, and long, long journal entries as an adolescent. Yet there also was always a harbored hope, and that was this: that writing might make a difference in someone's life.

Writing is like preaching—at least my preaching—in that I am never sure what will come of it. Will it connect with anyone or help anyone? Will it make any difference? Some time ago I preached at our school's chapel. To my students beforehand I commented that my sermon related to matters that we were studying in class, and I encouraged them to attend. On the day in question, I saw many of them when I preached. At the next class, two days later, I invited them to help me summarize the sermon, but they had trouble recalling much of what I said! Even though I preached what I considered to be a good sermon, it was a telling reminder of how unpredictable the fruits of preaching or writing can be.

Yet this book testifies to the fact that sometimes writing does make a difference and does have an impact. This is a revision and expansion of an earlier volume, *The Rhythm of God's Grace: Uncovering Morning and Evening Hours of Prayer*.[1] I wrote that book while suspecting that a kind of prayer that had been crucial in my own growth as a Christian for many years might be of use to other believers as well. I began that work while I was still a local church pastor and completed it when I was teaching at a seminary. Both were settings where I not only tested the theory of my ideas but also had many opportunities to pray in this fashion with other Christians.

The great and unexpected gift—a story I tell in the Epilogue—was that this book was one catalyst that brought together a remarkable group of people who quickly resolved that it was time to develop a book of prayers growing from and supporting Mennonite theological traditions. Within a few years, we were able to offer *Take Our Moments and Our Days: An Anabaptist Prayer Book* to fellow believers.[2]

I will no doubt keep writing, but I can say

with no exaggeration that the creation of *Take Our Moments and Our Days* is reason enough to have become a writer.

An Ancient Tradition with Current Relevance

I did not grow up learning or hearing about—let alone practicing—daily morning and evening prayer. Our family had formal prayers before and after each meal and a memorized prayer that we recited at bedtime. But no one mentioned or even knew that many Christians have set prayers early and late each day. Yet that ancient tradition goes back to the early church and still continues to inform, inspire, and hearten believers around the world.

Happily, we live in an era when high walls of denominations and traditions that once deeply divided the church are coming down. We benefit from, fellowship with, bless, and enlighten one another. More and more, Christians look to the traditions and heritage of the wider church. Once we were quick to dismiss the legacy of others: "Oh, that's just what those [other folks] do." But now we are more likely to learn what we can from other Jesus followers, whether Catholic or charismatic, formal or free form, liturgical or extemporaneous. Tyndale Seminary, where I now teach, has students representing over forty different denominations, and we hope to add a few more.

When I was a child, my parents often told me that one of the most remarkable experiences of living through the Nazi-occupied Netherlands during World War II was that Christians who previously were leery and suspicious of one another suddenly learned to care for and cooperate with each other. Before the war, divisions were so deep that Calvinists who look quite similar to me not only attended different churches and schools, but were also discouraged from dating each other and certainly from marrying each other. Yet shifts began during the war years. Not only different divisions of Calvinism cooperated with each other in the Resistance; even Catholics and Calvinists appreciated one another in their collaborative opposition to Nazism. In many ways, World War II set the stage for new forms of ecumenism, which were later bolstered by the Second Vatican Council (early 1960s), the charismatic renewal, and more recently the realization that the church in this postmodern, post-Christian era can no longer afford to compete against itself.

In claiming our deeper and prior unity, we can also look to earlier traditions and resources that other spheres of the church still honor.

Standing in the Need of Ancient Prayer

Years ago I found that common morning and evening prayer helped me overcome difficulties and weaknesses in my own spiritual disciplines. As a young adult, my prayer life was not able to withstand the crisis of the untimely death of my younger sister and only sibling, seventeen-year-old Margaret. While coping with that grief, I was first introduced to the possibilities of a prayer book. That discipline has stood me in good stead ever since, even now all these decades later. Common prayers keep reminding me that God is present, at work, and reliable. Thus, such prayers call me to pay attention and to trust that God is active, even when I cannot discern God's activity or even feel God's presence for a long, long time.

Later, first as a pastor and then as a seminary professor, I wondered whether this manner of praying could help others as well. I saw numerous people struggling with how to pray, wanting to do so but feeling stymied. I learned, however, that many had no idea about morning and evening prayer traditions, and little awareness of what they might offer and how they might help.

Yet, at the same time, I marveled to see people from various Christian streams embracing venerable types of prayer, both in ecumenical communities and in church groups. Liturgical traditions have kept such forms in existence for hundreds of years, but now many other kinds of Christians are also welcoming them. I wondered whether I could be part of introducing rich possibilities to new hearers and pray-ers.

Overview of This Book

This book explores what the ancient practice of morning and evening praying offers, why it is relevant today, and what prayer books such as *Take Our Moments and Our Days* promise.

In chapter 1 we consider basic understandings

of this form of prayer and consider why people are interested in uncovering such an old daily pattern.

In chapter 2 we look at internationally and ecumenically influential Christian communities, such as Iona and Taizé. Their morning and evening prayer rhythms are not only crucial to their identity and ministry, but also attract others to embrace such practices and empower the remarkable mission and outreach of these communities.

Chapter 3 shows that this prayer is deeply rooted in the Bible, both the Old and New Testaments. Such practices go back to the beginning of our faith and are a legacy that all Christians can still claim, celebrate, and share today.

What happened along the way to this rich inheritance bears exploration, and so chapter 4 examines the history of morning and evening prayer from the early centuries until now. Such prayer was gradually distorted and eventually lost by many (especially Protestants). Nevertheless, it still has much to offer all Christians, and those of an Anabaptist bent will find that they may have more affinities with such a tradition than they might realize at first.

In chapter 5 we consider how to understand this form of praying, so that we can appreciate its importance.

An aspect of our culture that gravitates against regulated prayer is suspicion of and resistance to discipline, especially in the spiritual life. So chapter 6 reflects on the paradoxical freedom of disciplines.

Still, such prayer is not easy, and thus chapter 7 looks at some of the hazards and obstacles.

Nevertheless, there are many blessings in this way of praying, as we see in chapter 8. It gives words to pray, sustains us in tough times, immerses us in Scriptures, helps us deal with the challenges of busyness, connects us to other Christians ecumenically, and supports us in our prayer.

In chapter 9 we learn about a small experiment with this kind of prayer and how it enriched the faith and faithfulness of the members of a church group, most of whom were new to such practices.

The epilogue reports the thinking, theology, development, and fruitfulness of *Take Our Moments and Our Days: An Anabaptist Prayer Book*.

To help you get started with praying in these ways, individually or as a group, appendixes include several practical resources. There you will find advice on praying morning and evening prayer, understanding its structure and content, and preparing and leading such prayer for groups. I also offer recommendations about several key resources.

I hope that this book will give you individually, or a small group of which you are a part, all that you need, practically and theologically, to begin praying daily morning and/or evening prayer. For those of you who already use a prayer book, such as *Take Our Moments and Our Days*, this will deepen your understanding of how and why so many Christians pray this way.

As I worked on this revision, I kept in mind the fact that the central purpose of the book had changed. In its first edition, I tried to provide everything that people might need to select and evaluate various prayer books. Given the publication of *Take Our Moments and Our Days*, that is no longer essential. This book then seeks rather to demonstrate the why and how of praying with such an aid.

Recovering, Discovering, or Uncovering?

Sometimes I've said that I want to encourage the *recovery* of common daily morning and evening prayer among those Christians (mostly Protestants, alas) who do not have it or do not know about it. The problem with that phrasing, though, is in its assuming that Protestants had it and merely need to find it again. But by early in the Reformation or soon afterward, most Protestants no longer observed such forms of prayer, although they may still have been unknowingly influenced by them. So "recovery" is not quite the right term.

At other times I say that I encourage the *discovery* of common daily morning and evening prayer. But that is not accurate either. Such prayer was never entirely lost, even if some discarded or discontinued its use. We can no more discover it than Columbus "discovered America." All along there were some Christians who knew about the Office and who still practice it. We do not discover this precious gift for the first time. At most we learn something that many other fellow believers never lost or forgot.

Thus the best way to describe and discuss this is to speak of *uncovering* common daily morning and evening prayer. Somehow a good number of faithful Christians have misplaced it, perhaps even buried it, giving it up as lifeless. Distortions, misdirected emphases, misguided priorities, and even good intentions gone wrong—these have gradually covered up and reworked the original genius of morning and evening prayer. Yet it remains there in the roots of Christianity, even within Protestant traditions, as we shall see. What is required, then, is not to find, invent, or discover something new. Rather, we have the gift and opportunity to encounter what is already there and to claim it as a potential legacy for all Christians. It is part of our heritage, and it can still be a great blessing.

I invite you not only to explore with me what happened to such prayer, but also to see what its potential can be for renewing our spiritual lives and enriching the life of the wider church.

Sharing the Joys

Near my final year as a pastor, I called a small group of people in my church to commit themselves to daily morning and evening prayer for the Easter season. Although this was new for them, most enjoyed themselves. As a result, in their spiritual lives several experienced more gratitude, a deeper awareness of God's presence, and an increased sense of purpose. Some commented on gladly learning the entirely new—but now obvious—idea of praying morning and evening, addressing and greeting God at these key points in the day.

As I grow more and more convinced of the gifts of such prayer, I long to share these joys with others too. And in that spirit, I offer this book—as good a reason as any to write.

CHAPTER 1

Finding a Lost Treasure
Uncovering Morning and Evening Prayer

When I was around eleven or twelve years of age, I began to take more responsibility and initiative for my own prayer life. Until then I had gone along with meal and bedtime prayers and Sunday worship, all of which were handled and led by others: parents, teachers, pastors. But I had a lively sense of God's presence. I never doubted God's reality and God's deep interest in me. So it seemed only natural then that I would want to talk with God regularly, to pray and read Scriptures on my own. As far as I can recall, no one taught me how, but I decided to do so anyway. Prayer has been important to me ever since.

For years I struggled to learn these disciplines by myself. I believed that such practices were important but was not always sure how to go about them. In high school I happily discovered and connected with other Christians who prioritized a "daily quiet time." Many of my new friends were committed to "devotions"; yet they also constantly labored to maintain them. We felt that we *should* do this but were not always as disciplined as we thought we ought to be or as regular as we wanted to be.

In university, I am sad to confess, I had little tolerance for Christian traditions other than my own. Once, on a whim, I rummaged in the discard bin of a local bookstore and bought a book by Jesuit priest Daniel Berrigan, a poet and peace activist. Mostly I intended to critique his faith and to figure out what was wrong with this famous person and his theology. I deeply disagreed with many things I had heard about him. But I had prejudged him and was in for a shock. I was startled to see that Berrigan took the Scriptures seriously and that his life, faith, vision, and activism were deeply shaped by daily prayer. I certainly did not agree with all his conclusions, but it was clear that here was a man who was rooted in prayer and the Bible. I also realized that his disciplined daily prayer was a far cry from the irregular personal devotions or daily quiet time that my friends and I tried to maintain. Many of us had trouble praying every single day. And when we did pray, it was usually self-directed and lasted for only a few minutes. Berrigan was more disciplined, far more disciplined, than anyone I knew. Then I realized that I had a lot to learn from other Christian traditions.

Through Berrigan, I first saw a deeper Christian practice of prayer and Scripture reading, which many of my faith companions and I were missing. Such traditional prayers are variously called the "daily office," "divine office," "common prayer," "liturgy of the hours" (prayers at certain set times), "morning and evening prayer," and even "fixed-hour prayer."

Around then, my sister and only sibling died of leukemia at age seventeen. This set off a huge faith crisis for me, one of the hardest things I ever experienced. Her death did not fit my cocky, smug, and self-righteous beliefs. I did not understand how God could allow such a terrible thing. And—this was particularly frightening—I also found myself unable to pray and wondered whether I was losing my faith. At times I had nothing to say to God or did not know how to voice my prayers. Sometimes I could think of things that I wanted to tell God but was not sure whether they were legitimate or blasphemous. So I clamped my mouth and my mind shut when thoughts turned toward God.

Then a friend showed me a Taizé prayer book called *Praise in All Our Days*.[1] I was comforted because that volume gave me words to pray. It helped me voice laments and also encouraged me to put my situation into a wider context. Slowly I learned to pray again. For many years I relied on that particular book.

Much has changed since I first skeptically read Dan Berrigan. Now as a Benedictine oblate, I am vowed to pray a version of the daily office for the rest of my life and have resolved some inadequacies in how I once prayed. (Oblates affiliate with particular monasteries, promising to live their lives in disciplined and accountable ways according to modified monastic priorities of simplicity, prayerfulness, discipline, and fidelity.)

But I am not yet content. I suspect that the

kinds of problems I have encountered along the way in my prayer life are troublesome for others too. And I have a hunch that morning and evening prayers might help many folks.

Standing in the Need of Prayer

When I was a pastor, congregants often said that they found it difficult to pray or told me that they had no time for that or did not know how to do it. It got to the point where I was actually surprised when an occasional person told me that he or she did pray every day. Such people were the exception, not the rule.

I am concerned about the inadequacy of our prayer, especially in a culture that bombards us nonstop in many ways and from all kinds of directions. Some may "pray" at most for an hour every seven days at Sunday worship and are at the same time formed by TV, up to twenty or more hours the same week, not to mention time surfing the Web or scanning other electronic and digital screens. Studies now suggest that each day many North Americans spend as much as twelve hours with electronic media!

Firsthand, I also know other difficulties of being prayerful. Before learning how to use a prayer book, my prayers were *ad hoc*: made up without paying attention to the Christian year, the priorities of the church and God's reign, or the needs of the wider world. They were *self-directed*: deciding on my own what I should pray rather than having help, support, or direction from others with maturity or experience, not to mention the wisdom of

Christian tradition. They were *disconnected*: prayed in isolation from other believers, both nearby and around the world. They were *subjective*: based on what I felt like, freely abandoning important modes of prayer such as confession, praise, and intercession. Besides that, when prayer relied totally on my own initiative and invention, it was easy to set it aside when the mood did not suit me or if life circumstances were overwhelming.

Such problems in the spiritual life can be addressed by a common discipline of daily morning and evening prayer. Though this may be a new idea for many, it grows out of ancient, long-standing Christian history and traditions. Whether we know it or not, it was there all along, hidden—as the saying goes—in plain sight.

The Significance of Fixed-Hour Praying

Prayer is about our bond with God and involves all that we are and do in the context of that most important relationship. Because this God connection is so significant, prayer needs to affect our whole life, every aspect of it, helping us to dwell and live in God's presence constantly and encouraging us to be faithful while doing so.

But how do we attain and achieve such a tall order? Christian prayer needs *discipline*. Authenticity, informality, and spontaneity are often helpful in the spiritual life, but they are not enough on which to base our prayer. Disciplined prayer has the possibility to inform our entire lives: what we think, how we act, and what we do. Various spiritual disciplines lend themselves to these priorities.

Just as discipline is important to prayer, *daily practice* is also vital. Most spiritual guides insist on the importance of praying every single day. Yet many people are unaware of a classic Christian form of daily prayer, probably the *earliest* form. For millennia, Christians observed regular prayers during the day and/or even in the night. The primary services have always been morning (sometimes called *Lauds* or *Matins*) and evening (*Vespers* or *Evensong*). Their history goes back to the earliest centuries of the church. Various versions of such daily observance—as many as seven or more services per day—can be found in Roman Catholic, Orthodox, and Anglican traditions, and there are Protestant variations as well. It is no exaggeration to say that for much of Christian history, this form of prayer has been vitally important—and indeed still is crucial—for many Christian traditions around the world today.

Such daily morning and evening prayer helps us pay attention to God and God's realities, what Douglas Steere calls "the deepest thing we know."[2] It embraces the whole of one's life. It offers consistent disciplines on a daily basis. Even its various names and labels are revealing.

Understanding the Terminology

One term for this kind of praying, "office," comes from the Latin word *officium*, which combines two terms: *opus*, "work"; and *facere*, "to do." "Office," thus, is connected with work, task, and even responsibility.[3] No surprise for us, perhaps: "going to the office" is a familiar phrase about fulfilling one's duty.

Fortunately, "office" has other connotations as well. According to *The Compact Edition of the Oxford English Dictionary*, its meanings also include "something done toward any one; a service, kindness, attention." I think of such daily prayer then as a goodness given to God, an offering, if you will. Surely God merits our service, kindness, and attention.

Another rich term for this discipline, "common prayer," has several senses. It means prayers shared with other believers, as in the Anglican *Book of Common Prayer* (BCP). The commonality can happen in the same place at the same time. Yet the shared discipline prayed in different places is still "common." In a real sense it is—to use a closely related word—*communal*. For years I employed an Anglican prayer book from a community in England. I never visited that particular place, but my prayers were ones that they shared with me and all others who relied on their good work. Now when I use a prayer book, I am aware of monks at St. Gregory's Abbey, the monastery where I am an oblate. I visit them only a few times a year, so I usually pray at home alone, but even then I know that I pray with them. Toward the end of many of their services, they recite a traditional monastic blessing:

> May the divine help remain with us always.
> And with our absent brethren.

They, too, are aware that others join them in their worship. Even those who are missing and gone are somehow connected and present.

Another sense of "common" prayer is that it is "plain" or "ordinary." This prayer happens in the normal, routine, and mundane—every day, no matter what our circumstances. It thus helps place all of one's life in the context of God's purposes and reign.

A third "common" connotation is from the fact that the BCP's first author, Thomas Cranmer in the sixteenth century, hoped that this kind of prayer would be again used by "common" people, not just the spiritual elite of priests, monks, and nuns. He asserted that this is a pattern meant for everyone.

Other terms—such as "divine hours," "liturgy of the hours," or "fixed-hour prayer"—remind us of a regular daily rotation of prayers (ranging from one to seven services a day) at certain set times. "Hour" here is not just time on a clock: this hour is more like a little church season. The hours, then, structure our days in a way that helps us pay attention to God and God's priorities.

Morning and evening prayers, as I have mentioned, take place in different Christian traditions. Sometimes the name tells you which one. "Common prayer" is usually Episcopalian or Anglican. "Liturgy of the Hours" is Roman Catholic terminology. The "daily office" is employed by Benedictines. (Benedictine does not automatically mean

Roman Catholic: there are Protestant Benedictines.) The "divine office" or "divine hours" tend to be Orthodox Christian terms. I generally use the terms "liturgy of the hours," "office," "common prayer," "divine hours," and "fixed-hour prayer" interchangeably.

This book focuses on morning and evening prayers. These classic devotions go back to the very beginnings of our faith. But they are not only of historical interest, not just a matter of being strongly rooted in Jewish and Christian traditions; they are also accessible and practical for people today.

Format of Morning and Evening Prayers

Even though different titles are used for such prayers, the services in all the traditions have much in common and are usually more similar than not. No matter the name, all around the world, every morning and every evening, Christians in churches, private homes, monasteries, schools, hospitals, retreat centers, and other communities are praying similarly. All these prayers are more alike than different.

A simple way to look at morning and evening prayers is to see them as having a parallel three-fold structure of first offering praise to God, next listening to God's word, and finally responding to God. (An outline can be found in Appendix B, "Structure and Content of Morning and Evening Prayer.") Praising God, listening to God, and responding to God is, or at least ought to be—the same threefold movement of most Christian worship services.

Morning prayer is often called "*Lauds*," which simply means "praise." Not surprisingly, then, praise is a high priority in this service. In fact, the first words of this Office are often derived from some variation on Psalm 51:15:

> O Lord, open my lips;
> And my mouth shall declare your praise.

In many places this is emphasized by making the sign of the cross on one's lips. Then follows an invitation to praise (perhaps one as simple as "O come, let us worship"), a psalm, possibly a hymn, and perhaps an opening prayer. Often, more psalms are read, sung, or recited. Those associated with morning prayer include Psalms 3, 5, 57, 63, 66, 92, 100, and 143. All are part of the first movement of morning prayer: praising and bringing glory to God.

The second part is listening to Scripture. Here there may be a lot of variety. Various lectionaries set different readings for every day of the year. If one reads from the Old Testament, this is followed by a song of praise (a canticle) from the Old Testament other than the Psalms (for example, 1 Samuel 2:1-8; 1 Chronicles 29:10-14; Song of Songs 8:7-8; Isaiah 2:3-5; Isaiah 9:2-7; Isaiah 12:2-6; Isaiah 40:9-11; Isaiah 43:15-21; Isaiah 55:6-11; Ezekiel 36:24-28; and Hosea 6:1-6). The Gospel of the day may then be read.

The third part of morning prayer is responding to God's word. This is done in several ways. We may wait in silence after the Scripture reading, allowing its words and meanings to sink in more deeply. Usually one next sings, prays, chants, or reads Zechariah's canticle, called the Benedictus, from Luke 1:68-79. It cites a morning image: "By the tender mercy of our God, the dawn from on high will break upon us" (v. 78).

After that come prayers of petition that focus especially on dedicating the day and its work to God. The Lord's Prayer often follows. Then the service closes with some kind of blessing or benediction.

Evening prayer, sometimes called "Vespers" or "Evensong," parallels morning prayer in its structure. (See appendix B for a comparison.) While praising is still an important part of this service, Vespers also guides us toward quieting down and being reflective—a fitting and appropriate agenda for the evening, as the day moves toward its end and we approach our nighttime rest.

This Office often begins with some version of Psalm 70:1. At St. Gregory's, the monks chant:

> O God, make speed to save us.
> O Lord, make haste to help us.

This opening response may be followed by a verse related to the time of day, for example, "Yours is the day, O God, yours also the night . . ." (Psalm 74:16) or "I will bless the Lord who gives me counsel; my heart teaches me, night after night" (Psalm 16:7).[4] Or see Psalm 139:10-11; Amos 5:8; or John 8:12.

In the first part of this service, it is appropriate to sing an evening hymn. A candle-lighting or light-blessing ceremony might be included. As in the morning, this is a place for psalms related to the time of day. A classic evening choice is Psalm 141: "Let my prayer be counted as incense before you, and the lifting up of my hands as an evening sacrifice" (v. 2). Other timely ones could be Psalm 4 or 16.

In the evening, New Testament canticles of praise are employed (for example, 1 Corinthians 13:4-13; Ephesians 1:3-10; Philippians 2:5b-11; Colossians 1:13-20; 1 Peter 2:21-25; 1 John 1:5-9; 1 John 4:7-11; excerpts from Revelation 4 and 5; 15:3-4; or 21:1-5a).

The Scripture reading is followed by Mary's great hymn of praise from Luke 1:46-55, the Magnificat.

Evening prayers then focus on intercessions, lifting up the needs of others. This too is concluded by the Lord's Prayer, and then people are dismissed with a blessing.

This pattern evolved over many centuries. When people refer to morning and evening prayer, they likely mean something similar to this. But why consider such an old and possibly staid or even outdated tradition?

Timely Reflections

It is now common to recognize our culture's current interest in spirituality. When I first attended seminary in the 1980s and wrote a thesis on the spiritual life, our school had only two explicit courses on prayer or spiritual formation. Since then, that very seminary began encouraging students to be both mentored by spiritual directors and trained as spiritual directors; it even offers a graduate degree in spirituality. (In fact, that is a program in which I eventually taught for a number of years, two decades after being a student there.) Times have changed and not just at that particular school—spiritual disciplines and practices, spiritual formation, and spiritual direction are almost routinely part of seminary curricula now.

Rising interest in spirituality is also evident in the growing popularity of books on prayer. This longing is not just a desire for the new; people are interested in roots and traditions. Over the last decades, book companies see that people are looking to classical Christian practices. In an interview with me, Phyllis Tickle, *Publishers Weekly* contributing editor for religion, observed how one publisher described this as "rapidly hastening toward the third century." Books more and more are turning to early Christianity, not just before the Reformation, but even before the church divided into East and West.

Uncovering morning and evening prayer represents one such return to ancient wisdom. It is praying in a way similar to believers who preceded us, and even a way of praying with them.

A Return to Ancient Monastic Wisdom

As a part of all this renewed interest, traditional separations are breaking down among Christians. Protestants now look to spiritualities from before the Reformation's sundering of the Western church. There is great interest, for example, in Orthodoxy, Franciscan spirituality, Celtic Christianity, and pre-Reformation mystics such as Julian of Norwich, Meister Eckhart, and Hildegard of Bingen, to name a few. Even Counter-Reformation-era mystics such as Teresa of Avila, Ignatius of Loyola, and John of the Cross now receive favorable attention from Protestants.

Whether this return to earlier wisdom is the cause or the result of ecumenism is hard to say. But the reality of such respect and cooperation cannot be denied. During a pilgrimage to England, Scotland, and France (which I describe in the next chapter), I noticed astonishing ecumenicity. Christians are bridging divides and uniting across former chasms. I now teach at Tyndale Seminary, a Canadian evangelical school whose students comprise more than forty different denominations—mostly, but not entirely, Protestant—and we do not hesitate to benefit from and study Christian traditions from around the world and throughout the two millennia of our history.

One form of pre-Reformation spirituality that receives increasing attention now is monasticism. This was already evident back in the 1990s with the best-selling status of *The Cloister Walk*, by Kathleen

Norris, and the surprising success of a Gregorian chant album by cloistered Benedictines in Spain. During my aforementioned pilgrimage visiting communities of prayer in Europe, I even learned of a Baptist Benedictine monastery established in England. In Minnesota one can find history's first United Methodist monastery (also Benedictine). And shelves of popularly written books about monasticism keep expanding.

Along with all this, there is growing interest in morning and evening prayer. In a conversation, Tickle told me that the "surge of prayer books" in recent years is highly unusual; she knew of no other time when so many were published virtually at once. The biggest publication surprise was a multivolume Office, *The Divine Hours*, edited by Tickle herself over ten years ago and still selling steadily. I often see it on the desks of colleagues, coffee tables of friends, and bookshelves of pastors. Ten thousand volumes of the pricey first edition quickly sold out. Tickle was particularly surprised by the interest of certain Protestants who previously preferred extemporaneous rather than written prayers. Her memoir, *The Shaping of a Life*, reflects on her own practice of fixed-hour prayer and how it has deeply formed her.[5]

Take Our Moments and Our Days

Overlooking such prayer is at the least a tragic disservice both for ourselves and the church. Given the long history of morning and evening prayer during most of church history and still predominating in much of the church, and realizing that it has formed the background of many spiritual classics, we ignore it at our own peril. We may love the wisdom of Brother Lawrence or Thomas Merton, Julian of Norwich or Hildegard of Bingen, Teresa of Avila or John of the Cross; what we must understand is that each one of these spiritual geniuses and giants was deeply influenced by their regular, daily observance of morning and evening prayer as part of a faith community.

Such prayer should not be an obligation for all Christians: Office practices have sometimes been harmed by such unhealthy demands. Even eloquent advocates of this kind of prayer admit that it is not for everyone.

Nevertheless the lost treasure of daily morning and evening prayer still has much to offer. This manner of devotion can help some—perhaps many—to pray. To paraphrase a great old hymn, "Take my life, and let it be": this is a way for God to "take our moments and our days; let them flow in ceaseless praise."[6] This was the lyric that also inspired the title for the Anabaptist prayer book volumes, *Take Our Moments and Our Days*.

CHAPTER 2

The Common Prayer of Uncommon Communities

Morning and Evening Prayer on the Ground

Though I had been using a prayer book for years in my own personal and private devotions, I eventually wanted to know how various Christian groups pray morning and evening prayer. So I traveled to Europe to visit communities that I had long admired: Lindisfarne or Holy Isle, Iona, Taizé, and Northumbria. I knew them to be significant places of prayer, retreat, and renewal. I appreciated their ecumenical influence and was astounded by their fame around the world. I went there to observe and experience their practices of daily prayer, to see what I could learn from them.

In short, I went abroad for inspiration and to test my hunches about whether common prayer still has something to offer us in our day.

Basement Praise

My first evening on Lindisfarne (also known as Holy Isle), off the northeast coast of England, I embarked on a stroll after supper and soon noticed a sign on a nearby building, welcoming visitors to "night prayer" with the Community of Aidan and Hilda. I had never heard of this group and did not know what to expect. Yet I decided to attend and see what was to be discovered. After all, the purpose of my trip was to explore people's common prayer, and here were Christians practicing just such a discipline. To my delight, I ended up liking the community's prayers so much that I attended services there each night of the week during my stay on the island.

The group ranged between eight and ten people. Worship was an unexpected blend of influences. We sang hymns and choruses, with the basses booming deeply and reverberating pleasingly in the basement chapel. Everyone took turns with Bible readings. There was space for personalized and extemporaneous intercessions. Once a week they practiced the laying on of hands for healing. Some spoke in tongues; others raised their hands in praise. I was delighted by the eclectic mix of Anglican, charismatic, evangelical, Celtic, Catholic, and Orthodox worship elements, a combination I had certainly never encountered in North America.

Who are these people? I wondered over and over to myself. At first I wasn't sure, but I did know one thing: *I liked them!* Later I learned that they were nationally known charismatic Christians who had gradually come to own and appreciate their Celtic spiritual heritage. My mystification about these hard-to-categorize Christians is a good reminder of one gift of fixed-hour prayer: geographically, theologically, denominationally, and temperamentally diverse Christians can be united by it.

After each service with this community, there was interaction among participants: sometimes simple conversations over tea, once a deep discussion about suffering and God's existence, occasional ministering to a particular need. When one person there heard that I was having trouble arranging a daylong excursion that week, she offered me—a stranger—the use of her auto the following day.

All of this confirmed that these services touched people's hearts and deepened aspects of their faith.

A Place of Pilgrimage and Prayer

Lindisfarne, as it happens, has been an important location of Christian pilgrimage for hundreds of years. Apparently Alcuin, a medieval archbishop and scholar, once told Charlemagne that it was "the holiest place in all of England." Numerous Celtic Christian saints (Cuthbert and Aidan, to name two) are associated with it, and also from here came a gloriously illustrated manuscript, the eighth-century *Lindisfarne Gospels*.

The island's oldest building, St. Mary the Virgin Church (Anglican), sees tens of thousands of visitors each year. Its architecture reflects both Saxon and Norman influences, some of it from before the twelfth century. Each day St. Mary's celebrates morning and evening prayers and communion. I enjoyed going there as much as I appreciated Aidan and Hilda. Knowing that people had prayed in this place for over a millennium gave me a strong sense of tradition and of the communion of saints. I love to worship between prayer-saturated walls.

I had not anticipated how cold this isle's location in the North Sea would be. Every day as I sat in that church for prayers, I wished that I had brought gloves and long johns on my journey, even though it was July. In each service the half dozen or so people stayed bundled up in warm clothes and winter coats. Yet I loved praying in this ancient structure while listening to the North Sea air howling outside. Jesus said that the Spirit is like the wind in that it "blows where it chooses" (John 3:8), and those gusts certainly reminded me of Pentecost. (One of Lindisfarne's earliest names, Inis Metcaut, means "island of the strong winds.")

Daily services in St. Mary the Virgin were "by the book," and the book in this case was the Alternative Services. Everything was according to Anglican common prayer traditions. Participants sat in the chancel, and each side of the choir took turns praying aloud a verse from the Psalms, slowly and meditatively.

When I was there, St. Mary's pastor was still David Adam, a man who has authored over a dozen books of Celtic Christian prayers and theological reflections, including *The Rhythm of Life: Celtic Daily Prayer*, an Office. He told me that he wrote that book for the many people, including Anglicans, who are unfamiliar with traditional daily prayer. Its short prayers and Scriptures can be memorized quickly so that those who use it may be nourished at all times and places, whether or not they have the book in hand.

Adam explained that since beginning his Holy Isle ministry, he's seen a "great searching in people." Numerous folks, he has found, want guidance for prayer. He enjoyed meeting as many visitors as possible, to offer them counsel, support, and advice. Adam encourages guests to go home and pray at the same time as the St. Mary's services, "so that they feel they've got a link." He also invites people to keep in touch with him by mail so that he can continue to give spiritual support. Prayers in his church, on this island retreat, become a foundation for offering pastoral care to many, not only when they visit as pilgrims, but also after they return home.

In Adam's ministry I saw something that was confirmed in each of the communities that I visited. Even though not all attenders went away committed to a full-blown version of the morning and evening liturgy of the hours, they were nevertheless attracted and drawn to a deeper life of prayer. And it was each community's rootedness in common prayer that helped give it important resources in its ministry of care, support, and formation both among themselves and beyond.

Humming Hymns and Cleaning Toilets

Next I went to Iona, another small island with a rich Christian legacy. This one is found off Scotland's west coast. Columba, an Irish monk, landed there in the sixth century and set up a monastic base that eventually evangelized much of Scotland, England, and Europe. The monastery is known as the source of a beautifully illustrated Celtic manuscript, *The Book of Kells* (from around 800 A.D.). The island's sense of history is further reinforced by ancient gravestones and standing crosses (one over a thousand years old). Samuel Johnson once wrote that a person "is little to be envied whose piety would not grow warmer among the ruins of Iona." It is a stunning place: stark hills, huge boulders, snow-white beaches, and many-hued waters.

In the 1930s, Church of Scotland (Presbyterian) clergyman George MacLeod gathered seminary students and tradespeople to rebuild the ruined medieval abbey. In this project, ministers collaborated with working-class folk while skilled laborers learned how to do theology. It was the beginning of the Iona Community. Now with more than two hundred members from many denominations, and still growing steadily, the community has a strong commitment to peace and justice and is known worldwide for its worship and music resources. Its weeklong island conferences are so popular that reservations must be made at least a year in advance.

I stayed at the abbey for a week. The hinges of each day were daily morning and evening worship. These times were of utmost importance, so that—as we were told at orientation on our first evening—the "day is held in prayer." The services were not optional: they were essential.

Worship and work were integrated. Morning prayer never ends with a closing blessing, since the work that follows is part of the worship; the evening service never begins with a call to worship (the customary opening prayer of such a service elsewhere), since it is regarded as an extension of the day's worshipful work. There is a strong emphasis here on sharing chores for the benefit of the community. Each day I went from attending morning prayers to cleaning toilets while still humming hymns.

Services ranged from liturgical and contemplative—evoking Iona's monastic heritage—to lively and inspiring, sometimes reminding me of revival meetings when we clapped enthusiastically to old gospel tunes. Singing included praise choruses, hymns, African-American spirituals, monastic chants, and international Christian music—all in the magnificent acoustic surroundings of the rebuilt medieval church. We prayed the Lord's Prayer (each in our most familiar language) rhythmically, phrase by phrase, every line echoing against the stone walls like the ocean waves beating on shoreline rocks a few hundred feet away. Prayers are continually being written and modified by community members in simple, vivid language, which communicates richly today but also taps into long-standing Christian traditions. Morning and evening worship, as practiced by Iona, is rooted in history but also is adapted for today's contexts.

Anticipating Heaven

During the hot July week that followed, I visited the Taizé community in southern France. There were more than 4,500 other pilgrims there that particular week, mostly young adults from many denominations and sixty nations (including a thousand from Eastern European countries). Summer weeks typically see between 2,500 and 6,000 visitors, with a total of over 100,000 pilgrims each year.

Taizé was founded by Brother Roger during World War II. Of Reformed background, he intended this to be a prayerful ecumenical community for reconciling Christians of different traditions, especially after the horrors of the war. Taizé now has a global ecumenical reputation, and its worship is influenced by many traditions, especially Roman Catholicism and Orthodoxy.

Taizé's only impressive building is the church—appropriately enough, the Taizé brothers would say. Every day is organized around three worship services—morning, noon, and evening, each lasting an hour. People sit or kneel in a darkened room, facing ceiling-to-floor banners, hundreds of flickering candles, and several large icons. Music is led by an unseen song leader and a volunteer choir. Each service is a series of Taizé chants, short Bible readings (especially from the Psalms and the Gospels), prayers (translated into four to six languages), and a deep silence of five to ten minutes (no mean feat with thousands of young people in attendance). In daily services the emphasis is on simplicity (especially necessary given the different language groups and church traditions) and on evoking mystery and reverence.

And it works. The music was so beautiful that for the first time in my life I was attracted to the idea of singing in heaven for all eternity, in spite of my weak and unreliable voice. A decade later I still remember the many songs I acquired that week: learning came simply by repetition. When the evening service ended at 9:20, many opted to sing and pray for hours more, often past midnight.

Clearly, some deep need and longing was being touched by the simple provision of space for daily prayers.

Intercession and a Leaky Roof

On this journey my last jaunt was to a much-less-well-known place, the Northumbria Community. Its symbolic center is Hetton Hall, an old rambling house in remote rural northern England, built around a thirteenth-century tower. I found the community to be friendly and informal, even a little amusingly disorganized. (The pay phone in the hall could not be used because it was jammed full of change, and no one knew where the key was to open it.)

Some years ago, a major publisher got hold of Northumbria's prayer book and sought permission to publish it. To this day, none of the community members could tell me for sure how that happened. But *Celtic Daily Prayer* sold well,[1] and as a result people have now visited Northumbria from the United States, Canada, France, Australia, and Russia. Community members are still caught off guard by the response to their prayer book and the ensuing interest in them.

I detected more of an evangelical flavor here than in other communities, especially in members' willingness to share personally and to pray for one another's specific needs. While I was there, I learned that an old friend of mine in Canada, Brian, had been struck by a car and was in a coma. Each day people inquired how I was doing and offered prayers for Brian, his family, and me.

There were influences other than evangelicalism. Everywhere I saw icons, and rooms were named after Celtic and Anglo-Saxon saints. The community is obviously enriched by a wide range of Christian traditions.

They pray together four times a day in a rough wooden chapel. Its ramshackle roof often leaks rainwater onto the hymnals. Their Office is liturgical with elements of Celtic imagery. They sing hymns and choruses. And there is ample time for sharing, especially of prayer concerns.

Visitors there told me of how Northumbria helped them in their faith. A Baptist member first found the liturgically influenced worship foreign but gradually saw that it affirmed "other truths, [which] I need to hear." She particularly appreciated the Office's connection with other Christian traditions.

Community member Rob Brown told me that

even nonliturgically inclined persons find "anchors" in fixed-hour prayer: "For people in deep struggles, to have something that happens every day at the same time is like a skeleton that keeps them from falling to pieces." When he said that, I remembered how important a prayer book was after my sister died and my spiritual life fell apart.

Northumbria is a place of ministry, healing, and growth. As in the other communities I visited, members feel a particular call to reach out to those who are skeptical of the established church. I have not been back to any of the four communities since I visited, but this is the one I most long to see again.

All Prayers Joined into One

More recently, on this side of the ocean, I stayed at the Monastery of Christ in the Desert in New Mexico for a week. It is in the wilderness, thirteen miles from the nearest paved road. This strikingly beautiful location is beside a river, surrounded by layered mountains.

As one expects in the desert, the sun was blazing hot. I certainly knew that I was not in Lindisfarne. But thick adobe church walls provided some relief from the oven-like conditions. On feast days, citrus-smelling incense wafted about, stirred by the searing desert winds blowing in through open doors. The Spirit moved here too.

There were usually a dozen monks or more, Asian, Latino, and white. Sometimes as they chanted they were off tune, poorly coordinated, and not in unison. But in spite of occasional fumbling, they always conveyed a sense of deep reverence and awe in their worship.

As I sat praying with them one morning, even though I had never been there before and it was a unique location, unlike any place I had ever visited, suddenly the entire service seemed quite familiar. This was so in spite of the fact that they often sang and prayed in Latin, which I don't speak. (I once heard Henri Nouwen say something to the effect that Taizé liked to use Latin in its songs because it is a language that makes us all feel equally awkward.)

While sitting there, I realized and sensed a connection to all the places in which I had prayed in Europe, certainly Aidan and Hilda, St. Mary the Virgin Church, Iona, Taizé, and Northumbria. I also recalled monasteries I had visited here in North America, whether the Anglican St. Gregory's Abbey in Three Rivers, Michigan (where I am an oblate); the Trappist Abbeys of Gethsemane in Kentucky (made famous by Thomas Merton) and Genesee in New York (written about by my spiritual father, Henri Nouwen); St. Meinrad Archabbey in Indiana (where I heard the best monastic singing ever); or the Cistercian Monastery of Notre Dame in Ontario (sadly, now closed). I vividly relived Vespers with Greek Orthodox monks in a remote region of Syria, and prayers in English, Coptic, Arabic, and Greek with friends at St. Mary's

Coptic Orthodox Church, near my former home in Kitchener.

All those experiences of praying and worshipping were joined together, no matter where I happened to be, no matter the language or church tradition, no matter even the different liturgical and worship styles. Reformed, evangelical, charismatic, Anglican, Trappist, Benedictine, Coptic Orthodox, Greek Orthodox, and nondenominational were all deeply united in these services.

It was not just that these people in each of these places were all Christians. Or even that they were worshipping. Their commonality went deeper: their services in structure and spirit were similar. They all prayed in the morning and in the evening. They used common psalms, canticles, and hymns. They regularly employed particular themes of praise, confession, and intercession. No matter their race, country, location, denomination, or liturgical preference, they had far more in common than not.

All these communities practiced forms of daily morning and evening prayer, a tradition that goes back to the beginning of Christian history. I long for a deeper appreciation by more fellow Christians for this rich way of praying.

Seekers and the Office

Christians in each of these places of prayer say that their common discipline of daily morning and evening worship is central to their worship, service, and outreach. The atmosphere and ethos formed by such practices is clearly also an essential reason for why these spiritual centers are widely influential, able to minister and draw so much attendance and attention from far away and around the globe.

Strikingly, Lindisfarne, Iona, Taizé, Northumbria, and Christ in the Desert are far off the beaten path and are difficult to reach. Accommodations are rough in these places. There are no shopping malls, video outlets, movie theaters, waterslides, or coffee shops nearby. Every day at Taizé I felt hungry, and there was not much I could do about that. Yet the growing numbers of visitors and pilgrims are astounding. People of all church stripes and even no church connections converge from around the world. Here is good news indeed in an era of spiritual searching.

Ray Simpson, leader of the Community of Aidan and Hilda, spoke with me about common prayer today. Like David Adam, he meets many people who come to Holy Isle seeking and yearning. They are, he told me, "fed up with churches that are task driven" and long for "something more organic, rhythmic," especially a rhythm of prayer. Yet, he observed, while many "churches are locked," no longer available for prayer, "houses of prayer are growing and becoming alive." There are more prayer and retreat centers now than ever.

I ruefully recalled Simpson's critique a few years later as I walked five hundred miles in Spain (a pilgrimage I describe in *The Way Is Made by Walking*).[2]

A large proportion of people on that route identified themselves as spiritual seekers. Many told me explicitly that they were not Christians. Often these same folks lamented that so few churches were open along the way. Numerous pilgrims wanted to visit. Some of my acquaintances actually entered every open church. Most of the buildings were locked: the few unlocked ones often felt more like museums than places of prayer and worship and retreat, sometimes even charging entrance fees!

In a time of pilgrimage, when people look to ancient Christian resources (or elsewhere when we do not provide them) and when they struggle with deep questions, the church must respond. Common prayer has helped form the many pilgrimage destinations described in this chapter. Such practices offer great promise for creating other sanctuaries too where people can find support in their prayer, and direction and help with their spiritual yearnings.

Though the level of interest may be unprecedented, these prayer forms are not. They are already rooted in biblical traditions. Since such ancient ways of devotion are dramatically relevant, we now turn from my twenty-first-century pilgrimage to the very foundations of these kinds of practices.

CHAPTER 3

Ancient Rhythms of Prayer
Biblical Roots of Morning and Evening Prayer

*i*t is amazing how long one can miss something that is right in front of your eyes. Growing up in Southern Ontario, I assumed that truly interesting birds were always and only found elsewhere in the world. I thought that all the local winged creatures were small to medium and mostly boringly black, brown, or gray: "LBJs" or "little brown jobs," as bird-watchers like to call them. I figured that colorful birds, large fowl, striking examples, or winged wonders must all live elsewhere, in warmer or more exotic climates.

Perhaps I was misled by reliance on nature shows and their easy revelation of intriguing vistas in faraway places. *Wild Kingdom* was a popular television program when I was a boy. Every Sunday night—instead of attending Sunday evening worship, the Calvinist equivalent of evening prayers—our family watched it faithfully, almost religiously.

Or maybe I missed out because of my lack of interest in science. On the other hand, I have never been particularly observant either. I have trouble finding my glasses even when they're on top of my head. And I usually don't notice when my wife gets a new haircut. So I had no idea of what kinds of birds lurked nearby.

As a young adult, when I lived in Indiana for the first time, I began going for daily walks through a nearby park along a river. One day a friend loaned me a camera zoom lens for my excursion, and I took it along and used it to look more closely at trees, bushes, and the riverbank as I strolled along.

My jaunt turned out to be a lot slower than usual that day and every day thereafter too, because I discovered a bird cornucopia that I had no idea existed anywhere in the northern hemisphere, let alone in the small Hoosier city of Elkhart. I saw iridescent indigo buntings, magisterial blue herons, improbably amusing northern flickers, colorful rufous-sided towhees, and stunning rose-breasted grosbeaks—to name just a few of the common and beautiful birds that I found flitting along the banks of the St. Joseph River. Some time later I happened to be in Southern Ontario near the neighborhood where I was raised, and I went birding there with a pair of binoculars. To my shock and chagrin, all those wonderful birds that I saw in Elkhart—and more too—were within blocks of my boyhood home. Yet I had somehow missed them while growing up.

Something similar happened to me once I started studying the discipline of common morning and evening prayer. It soon became clear that this practice is rooted in many familiar Bible passages, and yet I had never noticed it before. Other believers may also have overlooked some of the glaring clues.

Praising God in and through the Psalms

Christians have often called Psalms "the prayer book of the church." Throughout the centuries many different believers relied on this part of the Bible for prayer and worship, more than on any other biblical source.

In the church where I was raised, our worship book was called a "Psalter Hymnal" because in it all 150 Psalms were put to music. A good number of the pieces that we sang every week back then were based directly on Psalms, a practice dating to the early days of the Reformation. I own a lot of books, probably too many, but one of the most important and valuable ones is small (3 inches wide, 5 inches tall, 1 inch thick), with a sturdy nondescript leather cover, and its pages are yellowing newsprint. My great-grandmother's worship book was a convenient size so she could carry it to church every week, and its handy clasp closes the book firmly so pages will not be bent or tattered. The book includes the New Testament in old Dutch ("trustworthily translated" from the Greek, it proclaims), all the Psalms with accompanying music, other psalm arrangements for particular occasions (fruitful harvests or scanty produce, winter or summer, peace or war, church seasons or holidays, sermons or the Lord's Supper), and doctrines (God, creation, sinfulness, suffering, Jesus Christ, the Holy Trinity). I only know a little about my great-grandmother: she died during World War II as a result of the Nazi occupation. But I imagine her carrying this book to worship from home week after week, year after year, singing Psalms so often that she knew many of them by heart: opening this book was often merely a formality.

In the novel *The Thousand Autumns of Jacob de Zoet*, David Mitchell describes a pious young Dutch Calvinist in the eighteenth century who goes to Japan with a trading company for several years.[1] At that time the Japanese forbade all Christian contraband (rosaries, crucifixes, Bibles, and yes, Psalters). People arriving in that far-off country had to surrender their items to the authorities and could retrieve them only when they left. In the story, De Zoet has a crisis of conscience: he wants to honor and protect the Psalter handed on to him by his ancestors, but he also believes in obeying government authorities. Yet at great risk to himself and also to others (possible exile or worse), he chooses to smuggle and hide his volume so that he may employ it in his regular prayers. And not surprisingly, aptly relevant psalms come to mind for him whenever he is in crisis and needs the resources of his faith to sustain him.

Early in the last century my parents' Calvinist denomination began adding hymns that were not explicitly based on the book of Psalms; at the time, many believers, including my grandfather, were deeply offended. These other hymns were seen as being too superficial and not particularly biblical. Protesters in the pew would refuse to stand when those numbers were sung! In one guise or another, worship wars have gone on for a long time. Whether we agree with those who opposed hymns or not, they were certainly right that the stakes were high: the Psalms are central and foundational to Christian worship and prayer.

Psalms were originally the prayer and worship book for Jews, who still treasure it in that way. The first Christians (even before they were called "Christian") prayed as Jews. So they too relied on Psalms for their worship. To this day, morning and evening prayer counts heavily on that part of the Bible. It is common for many daily services to begin by praying one or more psalms.

These important texts do not just give us *content* for prayers but also teach us much about a biblical *understanding* of prayer.

First, the Psalms indicate that God is always and everywhere mysteriously available. Psalm 139 says that God is present in the womb, in heaven, and "at the farthest limits of the sea" (v. 9). God is immanent, to use a theological term.

Paradoxically, according to Psalm 139, God is at hand even where it feels as if God is distant or absent: in Sheol (the place of death and darkness; v. 8). In this connection the Psalms actually view complaining to and about God as prayer. One could not protest to God if God were missing or not listening. And the psalmist is grateful even in the midst of such anguish. Psalm 88 laments God's absence but begins:

> O Lord, God of my salvation,
>> when, at night, I cry out in your presence,
> let my prayer come before you;
>> incline your ear to my cry.

This most despairing psalm, possibly the saddest in the entire book, starts by prayerfully invoking God's presence. Psalm 73 details terrible complaints to God about injustice; the psalmist is in danger of becoming "embittered," he tells us in verse 21. But gradually he achieves an important realization (vv. 23-24):

> Nevertheless I am continually with you;
>> you hold my right hand.
> You guide me with your counsel,
>> and afterward you will receive me with honor.

Second, although God is always and everywhere present, there was nevertheless a sense among Jews that we needed to pray at *particular* times during the day (morning and evening), week (Sabbath), and year (annual festivals). The Psalms often speak of the priority of the morning, evening, and night for approaching God. Here, already, is early biblical evidence for fixed-hour prayers.

Faithful Jews practiced daily prayers at set times during the day (Psalm 55:17; Daniel 6:10). Many of us are familiar with how Daniel insisted on keeping daily fixed-hour prayers, even at the risk of being cast into the lions' den. Although it was against the law, Daniel would still "get down on his knees three times a day to pray to his God and praise him, just as he had done previously" (6:10b). The point of this story is not just that Daniel was pious or civilly disobedient, but that this Jewish practice of morning, noon, and evening devotions was worth risking his life. That, in other words, was no casual custom.

There is evidence elsewhere too of the significance of particular times. Temple sacrifices were offered twice daily by Jews, in the morning and evening. As well as praying before meals (another tradition that we Christians owe to Jews), Jews prayed twice a day, morning and evening, and many (like Daniel) also a third time, at noon. Each time they did so, they recited a famous text from Deuteronomy 6 (called the Shema [sheh-MAH]): "Hear, O Israel: The Lord is our God, the Lord alone. You shall love the Lord your God with all your heart, and with all your soul, and with all your might" (vv. 4-5). Many devout Jews still pray this confession at least twice a day. Christians, whether we are aware of it or not, inherited aspects of this tradition.

Praying Morning, Evening, and Night

I don't know about you, but prayer is not necessarily my first instinct in the morning. Usually grogginess, preparing for work, feeding the pets, and pondering the day's challenges weigh me down and preoccupy me. And in the evening, there is always so much that I want to get done, or I am just too tired to pray. But regular daily prayer keeps calling and inviting me to praise God: here, now, always, and everywhere—twice a day.

The Psalms show at least two reasons for praying at particular times. Psalms assert that we can know God's presence always only if we set aside certain moments to "pay attention to the deepest thing we know," one of my favorite definitions of prayer (from Steere).[2] The Jews did not buy into a more-current (and recent) notion that since God is present everywhere and in all times, we can forget about schedule and just pray anywhere or whenever we feel like it. Rather, they believed that regular devotions at specific moments help focus and reorient one toward God at all other times. They would say that *because* God is present everywhere and always, it is important for us to set aside particular periods to pray.

The Psalms go even further by suggesting that at certain moments of the day, it is actually easier to be aware of God. The psalmist often speaks of praying, worshipping, sacrificing, singing, or complaining to God in the morning. Psalm 59:16 says, "I will sing aloud of your steadfast love in the morning." Or look at Psalm 88:13: "In the morning my prayer comes before you." Psalm 5 says, "O Lord, in the morning you hear my voice; in the morning I plead my case to you, and watch." Suzanne Guthrie gives another translation of the first part of that verse, "At daybreak you listen for my voice," and notes that it is "as if the psalmist is saying that God waits and listens for that first word of prayer before anything else can happen."[3] That translation has a nuance of God's paying particular attention in the morning. Traditionally, as we have already observed, certain psalms are used in morning prayer, such as 3, 57, 143.

In the morning God blesses us in particular ways, and hence this truly is an especially important time to pay attention. In Psalm 30:5, the psalmist says: "Weeping may linger for the night, but joy comes with the morning." Even nature plays a part in all this, as we see in Psalm 90:5, where we are reminded of "grass that is renewed in the morning." Elsewhere, in Psalm 65:8, the psalmist speaks of how two junctures of the day are special messengers of God: "You make the gateways of the morning and the evening shout for joy."

In a delightful Celtic legend, Brendan the Navigator and his fellow Irish monks go on a long voyage and have many strange and marvelous adventures during their journey, perhaps traveling as far as North America. On one mysterious island, they encounter a flock of birds that sing psalms at evening and morning and at other hours as well: "Beating their wings against their sides, . . . they continued singing . . . for a whole hour. To the man of God [Brendan] and his companions, the rhythm of the melody combined with the sound of their beating wings seemed as sweet and moving as a plaintive song of lament." The monks are awestruck by the birds who "day and night . . . praised the Lord."[4]

What we bring to a situation affects how we perceive it. Once people assumed that birds sing because they are praising God. But now we are more likely to matter-of-factly think that they are just calling for food or fulfilling some other practical function of claiming territory or mating. Whatever the truth of the matter, I do believe that birdsong gives praise to God, as does the beauty of waters and wilderness, fields and forests, swamps and seas, mountains, and even, for that matter, molehills.

Is it just my imagination, or do birds sing more in the morning and evening? It certainly seems so to me, and one of many reasons that I love the spring is because I am often awakened by the sweet songs outside my windows. I much prefer to believe that birds are praising God, just as I honor the psalmist's ancient idea of morning and evening as gateways that shout for joy. What a gift in our relentlessly busy culture to see certain times as particularly rich opportunities to perceive or meet God.

Psalm 90 expresses hope for God to touch us in special ways at this time: "Satisfy us in the morning with your steadfast love, so that we may rejoice and be glad all our days" (v. 14). Morning is a key time to declare God's gracious relationship with us, as we see in Psalm 92:2: "to declare your steadfast love in the morning."

No wonder, then, that so much Christian emphasis has been on the importance of the morning, and not only in liturgical traditions. The award-winning African-American writer Maya Angelou wrote:

> During the picking season my grandmother would get out of bed at four o'clock (she never used an alarm clock) and creak down to her knees and chant in a sleep-filled voice, "Our Father, thank you for letting me see this New Day. Thank you that you didn't allow the bed I lay on last night to be my cooling board, nor my blanket my winding sheet. Guide my feet this day along the straight and narrow, and help me to put a bridle on my tongue. Bless this house, and everybody in it. Thank you in the name of your Son, Jesus Christ. Amen."[5]

The psalmist also speaks appreciatively of evening prayers. The "gateways" verse quoted above (65:8) reminds us of how times of twilight lend praise to God. The day's end, like the morning, the psalmist might say, is a moment of both blessing and hazard. Either way, it is a good idea to pray, whether to praise or to complain and lament (see 55:17.) Like morning, evening is a key opportunity for explicitly attending to God, according to the Psalms; many of these prayerful poems lend themselves to prayer late in the day.

The Psalms also make an explicit case for prayer at night. Consider this famous verse in Psalm 63:5-6: "My mouth praises you with joyful lips when

I think of you on my bed, and meditate on you in the watches of the night." In the longest Psalm, we see, "I remember your name in the night, O Lord" (119:55). Another psalm depicts this period as one of God's messengers: "Night to night declares knowledge" in a way that gives glory to God (19:2). It can also be a time of God's protection, as in 78:14; 91:5; 105:39; 121:6; 139:12. God often ministers to us then, says 42:8: "At night [God's] song is with me, a prayer to the God of my life."

Such nighttime themes are summed up in a famous psalm, 134:1-2, which is often used for night prayers, especially in monasteries:

> Come, bless the Lord, all you servants of the Lord,
>   who stand by night in the house of the Lord.
> Lift up your hands in the holy place,
>   and bless the Lord.

Jews said regular, daily prayers twice or even thrice each day. One intriguing psalm suggests even greater regularity: "*Seven* times a day I praise you for your righteous ordinances" (119:164). We do not actually have any other evidence of such frequent times of prayer being a norm for Jews or early Christians. But on the basis of this verse, monks much later tried to pray at least that often. Many still do. The monastery where I am an oblate is not at all unusual for praying at 4:00 a.m., 6:00 a.m., 8:00 a.m., 11:30 a.m., 2:00 p.m., 5:00 p.m., and 7:30 p.m.—an accumulation of about four to five hours spent in formal services. In other words they spend more time in church each day than many Christians do over the course of a month.

The idea of praying in the morning and evening or at night—even the substance of such prayers as they developed in liturgy of the hours traditions— is intrinsic to the Psalms. We can hardly claim to take Psalms seriously without considering fixed-hour prayers. But this is not only about the Old Testament, as important as that is.

New Testament Jewish Christian Prayer

Clearly the first Christians were deeply committed to being prayerful: "All these were constantly devoting themselves to prayer," we read already in the first chapter of Acts (v. 14a). Elsewhere we see that "they devoted themselves to the apostles' teaching and fellowship, to the breaking of bread and *the prayers*" (Acts 2:42). The definite article used here— "*the* prayers"—is at least "a reference to appointed times of united prayer among other believers" but also may well refer "to believers' attendance at regular prayer times in the temple (cf. 3:1)."[6]

Yet what do we actually know about prayer in the New Testament, especially as it relates to daily disciplines of the spiritual life? The Gospels show Jesus as praying both by himself and in synagogues with others on the Sabbath. He prayed at regular Jewish times: morning (Mark 1:35) and evening (Matthew 14:23; Mark 6:46). Perhaps the hymns and psalms that Jesus and the disciples sang at the Last Supper (Mark 14:26; Matthew 26:30) were Jewish evening prayers. Jesus, a committed Jew, maintained normal Jewish daily observances. He also exceeded them, often praying and vigiling through the night, for example.

Though we have some details about when Jesus prayed, he taught only one prayer as an explicit model: the "Lord's Prayer," also called the "Our Father."[7] Versions of it are found in Luke 11:1-4 and Matthew 6:9-13. In the Luke passage, Jesus offers this in response to the disciples' appeal: "Lord, teach us to pray, as John taught his disciples." Some see this as a request about *how* to pray. But Joachim Jeremias, an eminent New Testament scholar, rejects that theory. He argues that as religious Jews, the disciples would certainly have known how to pray. Jeremias asserts that they, like other religious groups, desired their own distinct prayer.[8] He says they wanted "a fixed prayer" and argues that the Lord's Prayer was actually the first Christian Office, a common daily prayer. This theory is substantiated by the fact that in the early centuries of the church, faithful Christians actually prayed it as an Office, two or three times every day. It eventually became a substitute for the Jewish Shema.

The book of Acts is also surprisingly and unexpectedly revealing about early Christian prayer. The disciples prayed together and in the temple and in synagogues, especially at particular times. In other words, they continued Jewish morning and evening patterns. Here again a careful reading reveals a fixed-hour tradition. This is often overlooked, just like those beautiful birds near my childhood home, or those neglected references to morning, evening, or night prayer in the Psalms.

People familiar with the Gospels or the book of Acts (especially older Scripture translations such as the King James Version) know that sometimes there are intriguing references to the "third," "sixth," or "ninth" hours. Without clocks, people divided daytime (however long or short) into twelve hours. The third hour was approximately three hours after sunrise, the sixth was around noon, and the ninth was associated with three hours after noon. These hours were announced publicly and were a convenient opportunity to gather to pray. In Scripture, these are the only times specifically and repeatedly associated with prayer. They were the moments every day when Jews prayed.

In the book of Acts, these three hours are explicitly connected to prayer. Pentecost happened at the third hour, while disciples were together, presumably praying (2:15 RSV). In 3:1, Peter and John pray at the ninth hour, "the hour of prayer." In 10:3 (RSV), Cornelius has his vision while keeping the "ninth hour" of prayer. In Acts 10, Peter has an amazing vision while praying at the sixth hour (v. 9).

This is more than a matter of people happening to decide to pray at certain convenient times. The Bible was written with too much care and deliberation for this to be mere coincidence. Scripture writers were not just careful time watchers. (Mechanical clocks that precisely measured sixty-minute hours were not available then.) And no mention is made of prayers at the first, second, fourth, fifth, seventh, eighth, tenth, eleventh, or twelfth hour. It is always either the third or sixth or ninth hour. The evidence strongly suggests that the third, sixth, and ninth hours had special significance and were important moments for prayer. Christians, in other words, prayed at the same time of day as Jews had been praying for centuries.

Indeed, Christian tradition grew more explicit in recommending prayers in the third, sixth, and ninth hours and tied such prayers to remembering the events of salvation. Some of God's most important actions (Pentecost, the visions of Peter and Cornelius) happened at these moments too. At the very least, those times were worth celebrating as mini-anniversaries of God's great work. (Now we might call them small church seasons.) Intriguingly, Gospel writers closely connected events of Jesus' suffering with these three key times of prayer. Jesus was crucified in the third hour (Mark 15:25). There was darkness from the sixth hour until the ninth hour (Matthew 27:45; Mark 15:33; Luke 23:44). Jesus cried out to God and died in the ninth hour (Matthew 27:46; Mark 15:34).

There were other variations on these times as well. One church father, Cyprian, suggested that the three times of prayer—morning, noon, and evening—should be connected to the persons of the Trinity.[9]

Themes of Prayer from the Early Life of the Church

In the first two centuries of the church, there were many references to prayer at these three fixed times. As the years passed, other prayers and services were added too. By the third century, authors referred to prayers as many as five times per day.

Certain themes emerge in these early developments. First, daily prayer was a high priority from the very beginning. Anna, who "never left the temple but worshiped there with fasting and prayer night and day" (Luke 2:37), may have been a model for this ideal.

Second, devotions were offered at certain set times. (Additional prayers were permitted, of course.) Morning and evening were strongly recommended, if not mandated. Such observances certainly included the Lord's Prayer.

Third, prayers were said both corporately and privately. People prayed together when possible. But even when apart from each other, they nonetheless had a strong sense of praying together, since their devotions had similar content and were said at the same time. To my mind, this is still one of the best and most compelling reasons for common morning and evening prayer.

Fourth, a persistent New Testament theme was "unceasing prayer" (Matthew 7:7-8; Luke 11:5-13; 18:1; Ephesians 6:18; Colossians 4:2; 1 Thessalonians

1:2; 5:16-18). Some argue that Paul's call to pray "continually" and "without ceasing" is actually a reminder to early Christians to observe the hours of prayer. "The command 'Pray constantly' in Romans 12:12 can mean: 'be faithful in observing the rite of prayer.'"[10] (The New Jerusalem Bible translates this passage as "keep praying regularly.")

So we see that the early centuries of Christian life and the Scriptures themselves provide us with ample reasons to take seriously daily practices of morning and evening prayer. Unfortunately, this heritage suffered setbacks and lamentable distortions in the following centuries, and it is to that sad history we now must turn.

CHAPTER 4

Where Have All the Hours Gone?
How the Office Was Lost

*m*any monasteries have their first worship service at 2:00 a.m. or even earlier every night! This middle-of-the-night or early-morning prayer derives from an ancient Christian tradition of worshipping and vigiling through the hours of darkness, waiting for God. So I guess we had best not call such prayer time an "ungodly hour."

The monastery where I have been going for thirty years or so is a little more relaxed. It starts at a lazy and leisurely 4:00 a.m. I admit that I find it hard to get to that particular service when I visit St. Gregory's, but I try to do so anyway because it is one of the most lovely in their entire daily cycle. In deep darkness, monks take turns reading Psalms aloud to one another for half an hour.

Monks traditionally do this in the wee hours because many Christians expect Jesus to return at that time, like a thief in the night. It's a form of fundamentalism on their part, I suppose. They want to be like the wise bridesmaids who can immediately greet the Lord when he returns. Even after the service, Benedictines do not return to bed; they don't want to be caught napping like the foolish bridesmaids!

Monks generally stop speaking after the final service the evening before, observing something called the Great Silence. They say not a word all night until the early service. Their first spoken words come from Psalm 51. After fasting from speech for a number of hours, they say: "Lord, open my lips, . . . that my mouth might declare your praise!" (cf. v. 15). Imagine that! The day's initial words are offered to God. Then the monks at St. Gregory's proceed to read the Psalms aloud, filling their mouths and each other's ears with God's praises. Talk about firstfruits living, firstfruits giving! How does that compare with beginning the day by opening a newspaper or turning on the radio, TV, or computer? Old, old worship practices still have much to offer us today.

Yet often when I speak about such ancient rhythms of prayer, whether in the churches where I have pastored or in seminary classes where I teach, people express surprise about this apparently new and unfamiliar approach. Many have never encountered it before and are not even aware of it. The simple truth is that an astounding number of Protestants have not been exposed to this practice. Or they have heard nothing good about it. When we see how important morning and evening prayers were to early Christians, this is astonishing.

What has happened to make such practices disappear from the radar screen of so many believers?

The Fourth Century

Nowadays we in the West often find it hard to gather people together for an hour or so even once a week for church. One pastoral colleague tells me that in his relatively active congregation, he never sees more than two-thirds of the membership on any Sunday morning (and attendance is even worse in the summer).

I once heard a well-known Christian theologian suggest that it is time for Christians to meet only every other week; that, he argued, is the realistic option in the face of all our busyness. I disagree: for one thing, meeting weekly is a long-standing Christian practice and, for another, meeting only once every fourteen days will likely spiral into even more infrequent attendance. If we miss one of those biweekly occasions, suddenly it's a norm to go to church only once a month. Furthermore, many believers from overseas whom I have met through my teaching speak of how devoted international sisters and brothers are to regular prayer, often gathering on a daily basis. Around the world, Korean Christians meet early in the morning every day for prayer and Bible study. They credit this practice with helping fuel the renewal of the church in South Korea. Ethiopian Christians are known to vigil all night every week from Friday evening until Saturday morning.

In contrast to Western Christians, who have difficulty finding time for one hour on Sunday each week, in the fourth century it was normal for most churches to have morning and evening prayer every single day, not just once a week. Many local believers attended and participated in such worship events on a consistently regular basis. Christian leaders actually expected and even demanded such involvement. Ambrose of Milan (339–397), for example, wanted all Christians to come to these services each morning. He considered such attendance a minimal requirement for faithful Christian discipleship.

Back then the church was not yet as centralized as it would become in later centuries, so the way the Office was practiced certainly varied from place to place. Yet those services also had much in common. They generally revolved around short excerpts from the Psalms, were carefully structured, drew people's active involvement and attention by simple rituals, and were short in duration, easily managed before the day's activities began or after a day's work and responsibilities were finished. These events were accessible, available, and engaging. But those qualities did not necessarily survive how the services evolved.

Monks and Prayer
During the fourth century, especially in Egypt, Palestine, and Syria, some Christians withdrew to the wilderness. These first monks were highly critical of the rest of the church and its clergy at the time. The Desert Fathers and Mothers wanted to abandon the corrupting influence of the world and rejected the church as being too comfortable. They moved into caves and simple cells that were exposed to a harsh climate. Such dramatic renun-

ciation also cut them off from the worship life of the wider church. Thus their morning and evening prayers unfolded in new directions.

Monks particularly longed to fulfill literally Paul's injunction to "pray without ceasing" (1 Thessalonians 5:17). Morning and evening services were not enough for many of these hard-core pray-ers. Furthermore, desert Christians often saw secular life and involvements as deterrents to being prayerful. For them, the wilderness afforded fewer distractions in the spiritual life. They added services to each day and spent many hours praying on a daily basis. Eventually some had up to eight daily services, including one in the night. There was some controversy about having fixed-hour prayers, however many there might be. One early monastic, John Cassian (c. 360–430), lamented that even having numerous set times fell short of unceasing prayer.

The way that monks worshipped was also quite different from the nonmonastic churches that they left behind. It was not only the amount of time they spent in prayer, but also how they went about it. For one thing, they prayed the entire Psalter in order (often every week, though some prayed all of the Psalms every day, an astonishing accomplishment). This obviously increased the amount of time that they spent in prayer. More significantly, the Psalms were no longer employed for corporate recitation and worship but now were used essentially for private and personal edification, reflection, and meditation. The Psalms were often followed by silent rumination, heightening the internally directed emphases of such devotions. This worship was geared toward individual edification, not communal celebration. Monastic services now were more akin to private prayer than to the corporate practices of other Christians.

Monks accomplished great things and continued to do so then and in the following centuries. In many places they served as missionaries, preservers of scholarship and wisdom, and teachers of prayer. We can be thankful for this movement. As a Benedictine oblate myself, I certainly feel a debt of gratitude. But in their services, ironically, monastics also moved in directions that helped divorce corporate worship from personal spirituality by putting so much emphasis and priority on private reflection. As we shall see, this began a trajectory with devastating consequences for the church's worship life.

Monasticism Goes to the Cathedral
Eventually some of those desert monastics started moving back to cities and towns. Church leaders there were largely happy to have such gifted, motivated, and committed believers nearby. So monks were often invited into positions of local church leadership. Gradually they shaped worship more and more in the image of what they had done in the desert. Their influence included adding elements to morning and evening services and also bringing in additional daily services. And so

worship grew longer, more complex to sing, and more frequent.

Corporate public worship that was once accessible every day to all was transformed. It grew into long, inwardly oriented devotional services that were available to fewer and fewer folks on a regular basis. Such demanding frequency and emphases were too burdensome for most people. This daily prayer now became more and more restricted to the religious elite—priests, monks, nuns—"professional" Christians.

Paul Bradshaw, a church historian specializing in worship, spells out contrasts between daily prayer before and after the influence of monasticism.[1] For one thing, worship moved from corporate emphasis to individual prayer. Previously, simple and colorful services involved the entire congregation's participation and attention, but gradually only priests and monks were essential. Laypeople did not even need to be present; there was no role for them except perhaps to observe what others were performing at the front of the building. Earlier worship had emphasized praise (via Psalms and canticles) and intercession. Now monastic worship, however, was subdued and inward looking. Office prayers were becoming segregated and privately oriented.

The idea of unceasing prayer was transformed along the way too. Formerly, when people gathered twice a day, it meant that their whole lives were regarded as prayerful. But many monks believed that unceasing prayer required spending as much time as possible in church, thus downplaying the significance or worth of those who were not priests or monks. In this understanding laypeople could not actually be truly prayerful; they certainly were unable to fulfill these new understandings of unceasing prayer. They were becoming second-class Christians.

Just a Cloister Walk with Thee?

Alas, in the Middle Ages, the tragic estrangement between corporate worship and personal spirituality deepened. Services continued to grow even longer and more complex. Furthermore, there was a gap between the official Latin employed by priests and monks in liturgies and the local language of many people. Most layfolk did not even understand the Latin services. Involvement became increasingly unlikely for laypersons. The long and narrow architectural layout of church naves made it difficult for people even to see what was happening in services far at the front. In fact, increasingly it became clear that their participation was not necessary, either practically or theologically. "Professionals" now conducted services on behalf of "lesser" or "secular" Christians.

At the same time, the expectations for "professional" Christians grew more taxing. Eventually all churches and priests were expected and obliged to observe eight Offices every single day. The demands of reading and praying so much Scripture, impossible for most folks, were even burdensome for clergy and monks. There were other complications: for example, detailed observances required many expensive books.

Increasing numbers of priests and monks recited the Offices privately, away from the local church, even though this had originally been discouraged. Meanwhile some mendicant traveling orders (Franciscans, Dominicans) officially stressed private recitation. Members of these groups were unable to carry all the prayer manuals and books, so breviaries (one-volume portable Office books) were developed. Thus morning and evening prayer became progressively dislocated from local gatherings.

During this time, many laypersons also moved away from corporate prayer. Wealthy people turned to private observance via beautifully illustrated Books of Hours, "*the* medieval bestseller, number one for nearly 250 years. More Books of Hours . . . were produced during this period than any other single type of book, including the Bible."[2]

People gradually found other alternatives to corporate worship: pilgrimages, Paternoster (Lord's Prayer) devotions, Stations of the Cross, veneration of saints, and the rosary. Individual privatized devotions meant that people did not need or rely on corporate worship and gatherings. Often when they attended Sunday services, they did not actually participate or even pay attention—neither understanding the Latin nor receiving communion. Rather, they just said their private devotions while in the congregation, mostly ignoring what priests and monks were doing at the front.

Movements such as the fourteenth-century Devotio Moderna (later so influential on many Reformers) built on these trajectories and emphasized interior subjective prayer and private piety. Corporate worship was increasingly being sundered from personal devotion.

Eventually daily prayer was no longer available or accessible to the church at large. In effect, it was only for those who lived distinct and separate lives in a cloister. The Office was now in deep trouble, and not only with the laity. Many priests found themselves more and more burdened by the obligation of praying all the fixed hours every singe day. Some newer orders abandoned corporate prayers altogether.

And even bigger showdowns were coming.

The Reformation and the Office

When Luther was still a monk, he grew quite frustrated with the daily demand to pray the Office. He would periodically get behind in this obligation and sometimes accumulated as many as three weeks' worth of unprayed prayers. Then he recited his quota without taking food or water for however many days it took, even when this practice made him physically ill. He finally gave up such daily requirements entirely when he fell three months behind in these duties and obligations. He was frustrated with the Office and not only because it was so time consuming.

Luther believed that the prayer books of his day had too much focus on fantastical stories about saints and too little attention to Scriptures. As far as he was concerned, God's word was effectively silenced by these misguided emphases. And such prayer, he believed, was being done as an obligatory work as if salvation could be earned.

After Luther decisively broke away from Rome, he did try to maintain a daily pared-down morning and evening service that involved preaching. But even this innovation tended to serve only clergy, seminarians, and academics; it soon fell mostly into disuse among his followers. As well, Luther created "house breviaries," private morning and evening prayers to be conducted at home, alone, or with one's family.[3] This is an ancestor of Protestant family devotions, practiced by my parents and grandparents and perhaps yours as well; but it is a tradition that is on the decline. It is certainly now less common for Mennonite individuals, families, or congregations to have common spiritual disciplines (morning/evening devotions, family worship, Bible study). Nevertheless, family devotional books such as *Rejoice!* and the popularity of online meditations show that not all is lost.

Other Protestant Reformers also tried to modify fixed-hour prayers. Some—Zwingli, for example—instituted daily services for his followers, hoping they would again serve the whole church, not only priests and monastics. In fact, the Protestant custom of morning and evening Sunday services is a vestige of daily morning and evening prayer. In Protestant innovations, local languages (rather than Latin) were preferred in worship. If music was employed, it was less demanding than monastic chant. Zwingli actually opposed having music in worship, but even when Protestant churches used music, fewer services were sung. The church calendar was also simplified. In spite of these innovations, Protestant devotions on the whole were relegated to the realms of pastors' studies, family prayers, or school chapels. Largely gone was the era of daily corporate morning and evening prayer with fellow believers gathered in a local church.

Anglicans were among the few Reformers to retain the liturgy of the hours, primarily via the *Book of Common Prayer*, which itself was heavily informed by monastic tradition. Thomas Cranmer, its author and editor, created several versions over the years, collapsing eight monastic services into two, morning (Matins) and evening (Evensong or Vespers).

Apart from Anglican endeavors, though, on the whole the divine office mostly fared poorly with Protestants. While we celebrate good things that have happened as a result of the Reformation and its needed changes, many people along the way lost even the popular devotions they had had before this impressive transition. The abolishing of "monastic hours of prayer, signaled by the church bell, removed the rhythm of frequent times for recollection," argues one historian.[4]

Too often, scholars tell us, many folks were now deprived of the vital practices of prayer that they had before the Reformation and never found a way to replace them.

The Reformation extended emphases that had already started in the late Middle Ages: "a trend to elevate individual, contemplative, and interior prayer as spiritually superior to the communal, external forms of the divine office, which it was thought could present a distraction to 'real' praying." This divorce between personal piety and corporate worship only continued to grow over the coming centuries. With the later industrial revolution and urbanization, people lost rural rhythms that permitted and encouraged regular prayer during the day. Individualism continued to spread as well, as did a voluntaristic approach to faith. "There were also the effects of the romantic revival and the resurgence of evangelistic fervor." Finally, growing literacy and mass production of literature made private devotional material more widely available.[5] Daily disciplines of prayer grew more and more endangered and haphazard, isolated and tenuous.

The Roman Office since the Sixteenth Century

Catholic and Orthodox Christian communities never totally lost the fixed-hour traditions. There were reform attempts by Roman Catholics and different breviaries proposed as early as the sixteenth century.

Nevertheless, the Catholic liturgy of the hours

remained as largely private prayer for priests and monastics. When laypersons were present at church services, mostly they listened, and often—even during the Eucharist—they said their own private devotions (for example, the Rosary or Stations of the Cross). Thus for a good part of the past few centuries, Rome also reinforced a schism between private piety and corporate worship.

In the 1960s significant work on revising the Office was launched by Vatican II. At that time the liturgy of the hours was revamped. It was pared down to be more accessible to and doable by laypersons. The revised Office was intended to better accommodate many daily lives by focusing on morning and evening prayer as the most important hours of the day. That long Vatican II process of reforming the liturgy of the hours also inspired many scholars of other Christian traditions to look at how the fixed-hour Office can best be applied and practiced again today.

Anabaptist Vestiges of Morning and Evening Prayer

Here we are particularly interested in how Anabaptist ancestors (forebears of Mennonites, Amish, and Hutterites) fit into this picture. Persecuted by both Protestants and Roman Catholics back in the sixteenth century, they usually had no safe meeting places to gather, so daily corporate prayers were generally impossible for them.[6] Their prayer life was deeply affected.

Yet it would be surprising if they quickly lost such venerable traditions. Many Anabaptist leaders who had been priests or monks once had a daily office obligation. Whether they recognized or admitted it or not, they were deeply formed by such prayerful practices. Other nascent Anabaptists were exposed to Protestant morning and evening prayers in Zwingli's church. Ironically, while Anabaptists idealized the early church, many did not actually realize that evening and morning prayer were well established early on; it was not just a "Catholic add-on" or distortion. All that they could see was how this tradition was not a helpful priority in the sixteenth century, and they simply but wrongly assumed that it was not well grounded in their Christian roots.

Yet even this radical tradition, which rejected so much of what was assumed by the rest of the church, showed remnants and vestiges of the Office's influence. The Schleitheim Confession, one of the earliest Swiss documents, says, for example: "The Psalter shall be read daily at home." This was possibly a direct "inheritance from monasticism."[7]

An Anabaptist leader, Balthasar Hubmaier, resumed daily church-bell ringing to call people to common public prayer, overturning the decisions of previous Protestant leaders who had stopped such a "Catholic" practice in that community.[8] He justified his decision by citing the book of Acts and writings of ancient church fathers that recommend the third, sixth, and ninth hours of prayer. He did see the connection to ancient church sources.

In 1534 or 1535 in Halberstadt, Prussia, in a small Anabaptist house church, "The brethren and sisters prayed four times daily, also before and after meals. They usually got up twice at night to pray and praise God."[9] This is a typical Office schedule.

Hutterites at first abandoned fixed prayers, preferring to be extemporaneous, but quickly moved to gathering for formal daily prayer, which they still observe to this day. This was easier for them to do than other groups because they lived together.

"In 1582 a defector said that in the morning [Hutterites] prayed, 'May God the Father protect me'; at noon, 'May God the Son protect me'; and in the evening, 'May the Holy Ghost protect me.'"[10] Intriguingly, Cyprian (third century) recommended linking morning, noon, and evening prayers to the three persons of the Trinity. While Anabaptists were radically innovative, their priorities were not all unprecedented.

Anabaptists began developing prayer books within a century. Hans de Ries published the first prayer collection by 1610 in the Netherlands. It includes prayers for every day: morning, evening, and before and after meals. A Dutch collection by Leenaert Clock was published in 1625 and later translated into German for German Mennonites. Non-Mennonite worship books were used as sources for these volumes.[11]

Some prayer books from that early era are still in print and in use among certain Anabaptist groups. Certain ones have been particularly long-lasting: *Ernsthafte Christenpflicht* (1708)[12] and *Güldene Aepffel in Silbern Schalen* (published in 1702 but written well before 1693), which have both been recently translated and re-released in accessible editions.[13] Many Amish still use a modified version of *Ernsthafte Christenpflicht* called *A Devoted Christian's Prayer Book*.[14]

Halberstadt, Hutterite, Hubmaier, and Mennonite prayer books point to an ongoing need for regular formal support in shared, daily prayer. However, although Anabaptists still strongly emphasize community, fewer and fewer have corporate prayer traditions. Even midweek prayer and Bible study meetings have largely disappeared. If many do not have time for Sunday morning, how can they squeeze in a weeknight as well?

It would certainly be worthwhile to study other Protestant traditions to look for vestiges of the Office. Family devotions, more common until recent decades, show traces of the Christian instinct for regular morning and evening prayers.

Yet one of the most compelling arguments that I know for common prayer practices unexpectedly came in world-famous headlines a few years ago.

A Startling Contemporary Anabaptist Example of the Fruitfulness of Office Prayer

As we are aware, lone gunmen massacre people with shocking regularity, often at schools. The names—Columbine, Virginia Tech—fill headlines and preoccupy the media for a time, but soon life returns to normal. There is almost an odd matter-of-factness about it all.

We respond to mass shootings with a feeling of "here-we-go-again." Sensational events briefly make headlines. Media invade for days of "in-depth coverage." We learn intimate details about victims and murderers. Perpetrators are scrutinized. Weapons are discussed. People do soul-searching about how this might have been avoided. Memorial services are observed. Then attention moves away, awaiting the next tragic shooting.

But in fall 2006, a group of Christian gunfire victims rewrote predictable scenarios.[15] This may well be the most famous event in all the centuries of Amish history. Although the Amish are often sentimentalized, exploited for tourism, or mocked by popular culture, they generally prefer to avoid or ignore attention. Imagine their discomfort, then, when within twenty-four hours of a tragic shooting at a small school in Pennsylvania, the Nickel Mines community was taken over by hordes of reporters, television vehicles, and media helicopters.

Yet those stubborn, plainly dressed folks were not overwhelmed by media, and they did not follow previous mass-shooting scripts either. Within a day of the tragic events, they let it be known—informally by word-of mouth—that they forgave the crimes. And then they acted. They visited the shooter's widow and shared donations with her.

They showed up at the perpetrator's burial. They observed that there was nothing remarkable about their forgiveness. They were just doing what Jesus commanded in the Sermon on the Mount and in the Lord's Prayer. *Forgiveness*—in all its strangeness, unpredictability, and inexplicability—suddenly became the focus of Nickel Mines media accounts.

What did not attract as much attention is how the Amish came to their matter-of-fact forgiveness, even in the face of atrocity. They reported that they had no choice because the Lord's Prayer asks God to forgive us as we have previously forgiven others. That petition is reinforced in the verses immediately following Matthew's version of the Lord's Prayer (6:14-15), which declares that our forgiveness by God is actually conditional on our forgiving others and that if we fail to forgive others, we ourselves will not be forgiven. The Amish here, by the way, make a connection that also was recommended in the ancient *Rule of Benedict*, where monks are required to pray the "Our Father" regularly through the day since it would help them live better in community by repeatedly drawing them into offering forgiveness toward one another.

The Amish regard the Lord's Prayer as the preeminent prayer available to us, divinely inspired, given by God. This seems clear and obvious to them since it was taught to us directly by Jesus himself. As a young businessman said:

We don't think we can improve on Jesus' prayer. Why would we need to? We think it's a pretty good, well-rounded prayer. It has all the key points in it.

I know many Christians, including Anabaptists, who look with suspicion on given prayers. They believe that only spontaneous and extemporaneous utterances have integrity and authenticity. It is only through them that the Spirit can move and speak, numerous folks claim. But the Amish see things differently. They believe that Christian humility requires us to pray primarily with the words that God gives us through the Lord's Prayer or via prayer books from the church tradition. Voicing our own intimate prayers could be seen as presumptuous or arrogant. Ministers do not compose or extemporize prayers. And during times of silence in Sunday worship, Amish congregants may recite the Lord's Prayer quietly, but ministers end the silent prayer by first reading a prayer from a prayer book and then by praying the Lord's Prayer aloud. For the Amish, set prayers are the norm, extemporaneous prayers the exception and almost never done in formal or public settings or on Sunday mornings.

Amish Christians pray the Lord's Prayer often, several times a day. They may not be aware that this practice goes back to the early days of the church, that the Lord's Prayer is actually Christianity's first daily office. Nevertheless they recite the words of Jesus at every church service, in the morning and evening every day at home, before meals, during family devotions, and on any occasion that requires prayer (for example, before traveling or during illnesses). This devotional practice is often the first thing that Amish children memorize.

As we consider the potential fruitfulness of "given" prayers, the Amish example reminds us of two important considerations. First, there are Anabaptist Christians who still stress and emphasize the significance and indeed priority of common, inherited prayers, whether from the Scriptures directly or from inherited church traditions. And second, even more strikingly, such prayer practices can deeply transform people. The Nickel Mines Amish would point to their embrace of the Lord's Prayer as a major, if not *the* major, factor in their startling act of forgiveness, a response that seems so unlikely that it even prompted worldwide mass media to stop and take notice.

Can the Dried Bones of These Prayers Live?

As we have seen, fixed-hour prayer went from being one of the most important ways that Christians worshiped and prayed for centuries to largely disappearing for many Protestants. And yet the witness of the Nickel Mines Amish reminds us that a spirituality of prayer by the book, one with "all the key points in it," still has rich potential and much to offer. Unfortunately, vital understandings of the Office were lost during the centuries between the early church and the Reformation.

To be sure, the Reformation responded to real concerns and corruptions. But along the way, Protestants discarded much that was worthwhile. This process threw out, among other things, the Office with the holy water, as it were.

Uncovering the genius of the liturgy of the hours could go a long way to renewing people's prayer and worship life. Common devotions might address particular problems that many of us face today in maintaining our prayer: what to do, when to pray, avoiding subjectivity and narcissism, connecting with the wider church, and relating to the church year.

But is this a reasonable or doable pursuit? How can we move again to taking forms of common prayer seriously? One important step will be to understand the theology, purpose, and potential of such practices. If we know and appreciate what they mean, then we are more likely able to engage in them again.

CHAPTER 5

Day by Day These Things We Pray

A Theology of Morning and Evening Prayer

orotheos of Gaza, a sixth-century Middle Eastern monk, tells a delightful story about early morning prayers in one monastic community. A spiritually insightful old man was praying with other monks when he saw a mysterious figure in glowing garments enter the chapel. The stranger was carrying a container of oil. At the beginning and ending of the service, he anointed all the brothers and even some empty seats. Afterward the old man approached this unknown person and asked about his identity and the purpose of his actions.

The visitor explained that he was an angel of God who was commissioned to take attendance at the daily office. When the Psalms began, the angel anointed any monks who were present from the start of the worship service! This action was a blessing that affirmed those who attended out of "earnestness and zeal and by their own free and deliberate choice."

But why, wondered the old man, did the angel also anoint some vacant places? This, the mysterious visitor explained, was because some people had legitimate reasons for being missing from the service. They may have intended to attend but became seriously ill, or the abbot gave them permission to be absent, or they had other official obligations that kept them away. So they too received the divine credit. Their absence was excused, not held against them.

According to the angel, however, unanointed seats indicated "those who were able to be there and through their carelessness were absent." He was ordered not to anoint those folks or their seats "since they had made themselves unworthy of it."[1]

When I was a pastor, I certainly appreciated it when people came to worship on time or even early. Nevertheless I am a little uncomfortable with the righteousness based on works that is implicit in this story. There are other obstacles and hindrances in people's lives that cannot always be overcome even by "earnestness and zeal." So I certainly would not want to connect taking attendance at morning and evening prayer with a system of divine brownie points.

Nevertheless, there is still something charming and deeply true about the image of receiving a blessing while attending worship. In the Christian life, blessings are seldom only one-way. We do not just bless God in our praise: we ourselves are also blessed.

What is more significant, this story also reveals how seriously common prayers were once regarded. Benedict of Nursia understood Psalm 138 to say, "In the presence of angels I will sing to you." Because of this, Benedict went on to commend: "Let us consider, then, how we ought to behave in the presence of God and his angels."[2] This concept may seem foreign these days, especially since so many of us know little about such forms of prayer. We have mostly forgotten those ancient traditions. To understand why the Office was so important—and still is—it is vital to explore the theology that lies behind it.

Morning and Evening, Our Praise Shall Rise to Thee

The first thing to recognize is that such prayer reminds us that morning and evening, the beginning and ending of each day, are not just periods on the clock: they also have profoundly theological ramifications. They have meaning; they can teach us and speak to us. We saw this already in our study of Psalms. We also sense a deep spiritual significance in the careful attention paid to evening and morning in creation in the first chapter of Genesis. Ancient Scripture writers understood that there was something full of potential and meaning at these particular times of day.

Is this really so surprising? In the touching novel *Walking Across Egypt*, author Clyde Edgerton writes about the elderly Mattie's morning habits:

> It was her favorite time of the day. . . . She also liked it when it was cold and she could stand there taking in the cold morning while the sky was red, and time stopped, stood still, and rested

for a minute. People thought that time never stood still, except in Joshua when the sun stood still; but she knew that for a minute before sunrise when the sky began to lighten, showing dark, early clouds, there was often a pause when nothing moved, not even time, and she was always happy to be up . . . in that moment; sometimes she tried to stand perfectly still, to not move with time not moving. . . . She hoped that when her time came, it would be close to morning, and she could wait for the still moment.[3]

What a lovely notion: "time stopped, stood still, and rested for a minute." This certainly rings true to me. We all know "early birds" who preach the benefits of rising when the morning is very young. When I do so, I am usually grateful. (But I am prevented from smug self-righteousness by recalling Psalm 127:2a: "It is in vain that you rise up early.")

Our experiences, literature, and art all keep reminding us that there is something full, rich, and even holy about sunrises and sunsets, the beginnings and endings of each day. Between Ash Wednesday and Easter Sunday, one of my friends made a Lenten practice of taking time each day to pay attention early in the morning to the sunrise and late in the day to the sunset. Most people recognize the beauty of such moments if they make the effort and take the time to pay attention. Those daily opportunities touch something primal within us. Thus it is not surprising that these two events of the day have often been key moments in different faiths through the ages, including Judaism and Christianity.

Many people have morning and evening rituals. For some it is juice or coffee in the morning; for others it is exercise in the evening or a snack before bedtime. I have heard that Hegel once remarked that the newspaper had replaced morning prayers. If we do not dedicate key moments to God, then those times, like anything that abhors a vacuum, will fill up with something else. How many of us load our day's first or last junction with the idle chatter of radio deejays, the latest bad news on TV, or checking email or tweets or Facebook or some other screen just one more time?

My father used to watch the news religiously twice a day, every evening after supper and then before going to bed. These functioned as antiprayers for him. He was unhappy about much in the world, and the daily news usually only made him angrier. I am not sure that he learned a lot from this habit or that he could do much about the distant events that upset him.

How are we shaped by the morning and evening habits that we choose to embrace? Does the raucous humor of early-morning radio edify us? Does hearing the media's daily take on the world's bad news before going to bed help us sleep better or have inspiring dreams? Or does it contribute to deepening despair and anxiety?

How do we steward such opportunities? Some

bow heads . . . over the daily newspaper. It looks almost prayerful. Some are mesmerized . . . by the glowing screens and brilliant and glittering images of the TV or computer. Their worldview is being deliberately shaped. Some go to a whole building full of people who are exerting, genuflecting, and prostrating themselves. Newspapers, TVs, computers, and exercise are good symbols of North American spirituality. But I doubt that they lead to eternal or abundant life.

Christian faith has long insisted that morning and evening are key times for spiritual growth and for being deliberate and intentional about how and where we pay attention. We are offered the option of being good stewards of those opportunities.

The Office keeps drawing and reorienting us to God's perspective. When I pray it, I see my life and my family being held by God and reliably entrusted there. As a pessimist, I find that this does not necessarily come naturally for me. But it does free me to remember that as important as any present reality may be, there is a more substantial eternal reality beyond it. As Jesus said in his first sermon, "the kingdom of heaven has come near" (Matthew 4:17b). In many ways, God's reign has already arrived, and I need to pay attention to it.

Just as some parents remind us that a hearty breakfast is a requirement for a good day, so wise teachers of spirituality commend the morning, the beginning of our day, as an important time for prayer, when we set goals and priorities to seek and serve God. Vital morning-prayer themes include praising, listening, and paying attention to God and devoting ourselves to God's reign. At the start of each day we commit ourselves to beginning again in God and staying attuned to God's Word and God's movement in our life and surroundings. It is a rich time to attend to the "deepest thing we know" (Steere).

Every twenty-four hours we receive another chance. A Desert Father, Abba Poemen, said: "Each day is a fresh beginning."[4] But it is not just an opportunity for us; it is also a gift that we present to God. John Cassian asserted that by dedicating morning time to prayer, we actually give God our day's firstfruits.[5] Remember that the term "Office" is related to offering. Praying at such junctures makes our whole life a sacrifice of praise, one that gives glory to God.

Similarly, at day's end we review what has happened, see where we have encountered God, confess where we have let God down, and relinquish all into God's hands. Important themes of evening prayers include praise, confession, and release to God.

The deep theological nature of evening and morning is spelled out by Eugene Peterson. He reminds us that the Jewish day actually begins in the evening:

> The Hebrew evening/morning sequence conditions us to the rhythms of grace. We go to sleep,

and God begins [God's] work. As we sleep, [God] develops [God's] covenant. We wake and are called out to participate in God's creative action. We respond in faith, in work. But always grace is previous. Grace is primary. We wake into a world we didn't make, into a salvation we didn't earn. Evening: God begins, without our help, [God's] creative day. Morning: God calls us to enjoy and share and develop the work [that God] initiated. Creation and covenant are sheer grace and there to greet us every morning.[6]

The way we enter and leave each morning and evening affects every twenty-four-hour journey. Our day becomes a pilgrimage that revolves around these two ellipses. Psalm 65:8 reminds us that these key moments are special messengers of God: "You make the gateways of the morning and the evening shout for joy."

Evening and morning prayers reflect a central Christian truth, what some theologians call the paschal mystery: life comes from the death and resurrection of Jesus Christ. Similarly, we are called to die to our old selves and to sin, and to take up our cross so that we too might know new and eternal life and be born again. In this perspective, evening prayer is a small death; we surrender ourselves into God's hands. Think, then, of the appropriateness of that classic but oddly unsettling children's prayer: "If I should die before I wake. . . ." The morning is a small rebirth and resurrection. We often give thanks for a new day and its opportunities. Recall the traditional African-American prayer of Maya Angelou's grandmother (in chap. 3): "Our Father, thank you for letting me see this New Day. Thank you that you didn't allow the bed I lay on last night to be my cooling board, nor my blanket my winding sheet." The dying and rising are relived in each daily cycle. Thus, as we observe evening and morning rhythms, we also have opportunity to live deeply and enter into the most basic and important truths of our faith.

The Office keeps reminding us of God's eternally trustworthy and reliable realities, no matter what. Some time ago I went to bed discouraged and spent the night sleepless because of some bad news I had heard that evening. The next day I got up with the sun for a vigorous bicycle ride in a nearby forest. All was quiet, peaceful, still, and beautiful. The air was clear and cool. I could hear birds singing. In those early moments I experienced the refreshment that also often occurs as I pray the Office. I knew then that even while some circumstances certainly are bad, the world is still a place of much beauty, and God is always to be trusted.

Sanctification of Time

Wanting to grow spiritually I have occasionally asked for counsel on living faithfully from trusted mentors: Henri Nouwen, a significant mentor for me when he was alive (1932–96), and later Abbot Andrew Marr, who guides me as an oblate. Both have helped me. The first point they ever told me was precisely the same: every single day I have to set apart regular times to focus on God and the things of God.

For humans, there are basic, mundane challenges that are nevertheless so vitally important that they need to happen every twenty-four hours: brushing and flossing teeth, washing our bodies, exercising, taking vitamins, and eating balanced meals. Spiritual masters teach that prayer is an essential requirement that must be met at least once every day.

Such priorities are easy to overlook. Less and less are we exposed to the old tradition of local church bells ringing regularly through the day as a call to prayer. George Herbert was a famously devout and attentive Anglican pastor in an early seventeenth-century English parish. Izaak Walton, a seventeenth-century writer best known for *The Compleat Angler*, was one of Herbert's first biographers. He reported that Herbert's public observance of daily morning and evening Offices drew in many from the area. This priest always let church bells ring at the beginning of the service, and local folks who could not attend would nevertheless pause and pray when they heard the pealing; even farmers and those working in the fields "would let their Plow rest when Mr. Herbert's . . . bell rung to prayers, that they might also offer their devotions to God with [Herbert]."[7] Formerly familiar bells were intended to remind us of God's presence and to call us to prayer when we heard them.

Brother Abraham of St. Gregory's Abbey writes of his monastery's bell, which calls monks to prayer, meals, work, and leisure. He names it the "monk's best friend." Such reminders may sound simple, but even they can be a surprisingly difficult discipline, as Brother Abraham observes. "They make it clear to me that as a monk, I am to possess nothing—even my time is not my own."[8]

When I visited the Monastery of Christ in the Desert, Brother Isaac, then the assistant guestmaster, told me that John Wesley committed five minutes every hour to prayer. (How delightful that a devout Roman Catholic monk instructed a Mennonite pastor in Methodist prayer practices!) Wesley also spoke of giving an hour a day and a day a week to God.

In a similar spirit, I once set my computer to chime every fifteen minutes, thinking that this device could summon me to pause and pray for a few moments whenever I heard it. Even though it was my idea, I found myself incredibly resistant to the intrusion and sometimes resentful about it. Yet how much more worshipful and appropriate such interruptions are than watches that beep or cell phones that ring during worship services. Such disruptions are hardly a reverent call to prayer. Rather, they usually just make us anxious, reminding us that "precious time is slipping away," as Van Morrison sings.

Praying regularly throughout the day is not always easy, but most spiritual masters urge us to find ways of doing so. Although morning and evening are key opportunities for this, we also know that careers, life stages, family situations, and varied responsibilities do not always make this consistently possible. When our children were small and I stayed home with them, I could not count on regular times to plan and schedule my daily prayers; I just prayed whenever Erin and Paul conked out and took their naps!

In our day and age we all need other ways of looking at and dealing with the movement of the clock. Time can be a place to meet God and to receive God's blessings (like the monastics in Dorotheos's story, perhaps). Meeting God in our lives, in the flow of our life, is a good way to speak of the sanctification of time, making holy both day and night. "Sanctify" means "to make holy." Many experience time as fleeting, rare, endangered, and even oppressive; but it can also be turned into divine opportunity for paying attention to God. "Christian practices for opening the gift of time resist the inhumane rhythms that shape so much of contemporary life."[9]

Another way to speak of this idea is "redeeming the time" (KJV) or "making the most of the time," terms from Paul (Ephesians 5:16; Colossians 4:5). Sanctifying, redeeming, and making the most of time means living our lives from and in God's eternal perspective.

As a pastor, I saw that our experience of time today is actually a huge spiritual problem. Our Christian and Jewish heritage recommends seeing and living in time differently by regularly and consistently prioritizing daily prayer, weekly Sabbaths, religious feasts, liturgical seasons, and sabbatical and Jubilee years. Yet many of us no longer know how to do that.

The challenge is not that time is profane and thus we try to force it to be holy. Rather, it is a sphere where we can encounter the holy and where we ourselves can be holy. Yet too often we sully and profane it instead. "Sanctifying" literally means "setting apart." In morning and evening prayer, we set aside certain times, hours, and moments to pray, sanctifying them by interrupting our regular schedules. In so doing, we resist and even break the tyranny of time, whether it be the agenda of others or our own compulsions and misplaced priorities.

Not only set-apart times, interruptions, and interventions are holy. Rather, we put to one side some time to pray, pay attention to God, listen to God, and focus on God's priorities so that all of life can be holy. Theologian Heather Murray Elkins has a marvelous term; she speaks of "altaring time."[10] Her pun suggests both the offering of time to God and the fact that such sacrifice alters, changes, and makes holy our experience of time. We praise God in specific moments of prayer so that we might praise God at all times.

Sixteenth-century Anabaptist ancestors in the faith were rightly concerned that too many churches confined and restricted God's presence to certain especially "holy" times, places, or people. Our problem today, however, is far different than theirs. Our world presents the real danger that people cannot find God at all in any time, any place, or any person. Setting aside moments in our day is a way to overcome this challenge.

Offering time is an important sacrifice. It is one of the most precious things we have to give. Time is a rare commodity and often feels particularly endangered in our culture. Giving time, sacrificing and "altaring" it, is a basic act of worship and praise. Just as giving our money helps us exercise discernment about how we spend all our earnings, offering time also helps us make careful choices and decisions about how we pass the rest of our time.

A vital goal of fixed-hour prayer is to make us always aware of God, to be present to God, and to be mindful of God's presence in time, aware of the "sanctification of time." After all, "the kingdom of heaven has come near," even into our experience. In this way we begin to practice Paul's ideal of unceasing prayer when our whole lives are experienced in the context of our existence in God, when we live as faithful to God and God's reign, and when we bring all of our circumstances into our ongoing conversation with God, always paying "attention to the deepest things we know" (Steere).

Some complain that this kind of regular prayer might be boring or repetitive. It's certainly true that it does not always ignite emotional fireworks, mystical revelations, or ecstatic experiences. But the mundane aspects of the Office are also essential for sanctifying our ordinary lives and for reminding us that God is ultimately and often found in the plain and the routine, more than in the extraordinary and the melodramatic. The ordinariness, everydayness, and routine aspects of the Office help us appreciate God in all of our life, including its humdrum and repetitive rhythms.

Sanctifying time is emphasized in Iona daily prayers. That's how worship and work are integrated there. At the end of the morning service, there is a brief but telling rubric: "We remain standing to leave, the work of our day flowing directly from our worship." It was not just a quirky happenstance that Iona services left me humming hymns while cleaning bathrooms.

The Office as Spiritual Orientation

When I was a pastor, every week I was involved in many different activities: leading worship, preaching, teaching Sunday school, attending committee meetings, visiting congregants, and addressing conflicts. At times these foci and roles and responsibilities could feel disconnected, but I knew they all had something vital in common. Each and every one was intended to help people seek and pay attention to God. As we saw in our reflections on the sanctification of time, we are called to turn toward God in all of our lives and activities. That is a priority for every Christian, everyone who is baptized, not just pastors or other "professional Christians" or those in so-called full-time ministry.

On Sundays and in our daily prayer, we test our directions against the dimensions of God's reign. In such moments, we may see the need to readjust. Then God's reality and priorities inform us, each day, both in mundane life and in difficult crises. We all need ongoing orientation and reorientation in this hard work.

"Orient" originally was a noun meaning "east." It eventually became a verb, one that was explicitly related to worship. It meant arranging or aligning a church sanctuary to face east, an ancient Christian tradition. Believers thought that when Jesus returned, he would appear in the east, so worship spaces were set up accordingly and thus ancient traditions have church buildings face east. The word "orient" now has other connotations as well. Orienteering is a sport of finding one's way through difficult territory or wilderness by using only a map or a compass. Both "orient" and "orienteering" are terms that demand action, not just attitude or awareness. It is not enough to turn one's gaze or attention to God in theory: One needs to rework and redirect one's whole life that way. Spiritual orienting calls for people to integrate mind, heart, and hand into the life to which God calls us.

Morning and evening prayer are major means of orientation for us: "As the scanning ray of the radar screen shows up objects in regular flashes, the daily prayers regularly flash up a matrix which we put against the world in which we live our daily lives, and this gives us orientation, so that we discover where we are."[11]

Daily morning and evening prayer provides a regular opportunity to be oriented by and to God's true light. But this is no solo enterprise.

Communion of Saints

When I was twenty, my seventeen-year-old sister died of complications connected to leukemia. Being cut off from her felt unbearable. Yet even in my deepest grief, I believed that she still existed in some way. She was no longer alive and present to us, but I never stopped being convinced that she had not totally disappeared. She was with God, in God's loving presence. So sometimes when I prayed, I even asked God to greet her.

When I was thirty-four, my father died of cancer at age sixty-three. He'd had three heart attacks, and this was his third cancer diagnosis. I was not surprised that he was gone, but I was very sad about it. Soon I had the strong sense that he could see me, that he was looking on approvingly, even as a cheerleader. (The idea of my father—a serious and dour man who loathed physical exercise—being a cheerleader is amusing on several counts.) His body was gone from us, but he was not completely absent.

In both instances, I was experiencing what Christians call the communion of saints. All of God's beloved, alive and dead, are held in God's love, present to God, and significantly present to one another and even in mysterious ways to us. Being mindful of all the faithful people who preceded us, we too are encouraged and heartened to keep the faith. As the Scripture says in Hebrews 12:1-2, "Therefore, since we are surrounded by so great a cloud of witnesses, let us also lay aside every weight and the sin that clings so closely, and let us run with perseverance the race that is set before us." The cheerleading metaphor also works well here.

Common prayer is a vivid way of participating in the communion of the saints. Earlier I wrote about being at the Monastery of Christ in the Desert, where suddenly prayers that I had prayed in many different contexts, settings, and places were all joined into one. That too was an experience of the communion of saints.

Prayer brings unexpected, unlikely—and some would even say impossible—connections, defying normal boundaries and limitations of time and space.

A friend was serving a life sentence in prison. For years he received cassette tapes of our congregation's worship services. At first he just longed to hear sermons and was loyal to me, his friend the preacher. Then along the way he asked for bulletins and a hymnal so that he could follow along with the prayers and hymns too. Because we sent a package every four weeks and the prison was slow in delivering mail, he often did not hear the tapes until several months later. Even so, this friend—who is not Mennonite—did not just listen to the tapes but also sang and prayed along with the Bloomingdale Mennonite Church . . . months later.

This example shows that the communion of saints operates not only outside the limits of geography and space, but also beyond boundaries of time. It connects all Christians everywhere who have ever lived. This prisoner prayed with our congregation even though chronologically he did not join in until months later. In a real way we were united.

The communion of saints offers a powerful transcendence. An Orthodox Christian, Anatoli Levetin, was also an inmate. He was imprisoned in the Soviet Union for providing religious education for youth. During his solitary confinement, his daily prayer was the Orthodox Office.

> I would begin walking round my cell, repeating its words to myself. I was then inseparably linked to the whole Christian world. In the Great Litany I would always pray for the Pope and for the Oecumenical Patriarch, as well as for the leaders of my own church. . . . I felt myself standing before the face of the Lord, sensing almost physically his wounded, bleeding body. I would begin praying in my own words, remembering all those near to me, those in prison and those who were free, those still alive and those who had died. More and more names welled up from my memory. . . . The prison walls moved apart and the whole universe became my residence, visible, and invisible, the universe for which that wounded, pierced body offered itself in sacrifice.[12]

The daily office is composed of texts and emphases that the church has prayed throughout the ages and around the world. Those prayers will be lifted up by the faithful until the end of time, and we may even expect to say them in the coming fulfillment of the kingdom as well. Whenever we pray them, we join the whole communion of saints, present and absent and future, here and gone and still to come.

In an age and culture of individualism gone seriously awry, such common prayer calls us into a broader solidarity, community, and fellowship that helps each one of us live faithfully in God's reign.

Roll Call? Role Call?

Do you remember how teachers took attendance or roll call first thing during our elementary-school years? Roll call is partly an administrative function. School grades and government funding have some relationship to attendance. Yet there are other reasons for such practices. Schoolteachers tell me that it is not just that the administrators need to know who is there that day but also that the authorities want their pupils to remember who is in charge. Roll call reminds students of their responsibilities, accountability, and yes, if you'll forgive the pun, *roles*.

Now God is not a divine schoolmaster who carefully tracks our every move, rewarding good attendance (despite Dorotheos of Gaza's story about the angel), intimidating us, and punishing us for being tardy or absent. Christian faith is not about winning or earning salvation by performing externally imposed legalities.

Nevertheless we know that attendance is important. Woody Allen said that "90 percent of life is just showing up." Being there, being present, remaining faithful to commitments—all these are vital. Even if we sometimes are routine in fulfilling our duties, they can still be important. I once read a study of marriages that survived and even thrived over the years, and the one thing that they all had in common was not compatibility, communication, counseling, regular dates, or mind-blowing sex, but the simple fact that the partners kissed each other every morning and night. Nothing was said about how much passion or authenticity went into those little rituals. Apparently even perfunctory pecks could be powerful. Think, then, of common prayer as a good-morning and good-evening kiss.

The ritual of roll call can speak to us on deep levels. When controversy raged around whether the Lord's Prayer should be prayed in public schools, one teacher friend of mine, a serious Christian, argued with great passion that, yes, the Lord's Prayer should be mandatory because this was a crucial way to quiet pupils at the start of the day. I disagree about such a use of Christian prayer but now see that schoolteachers used roll calls as a way of slowing us students down from the excitement and noise we brought in from before classes or from rowdy recesses. It was a reminder to us of who we were (students) and where (in school). It was a role call, having to do with identity and responsibility.

When we pray morning and evening prayer, praise God, hear Scriptures, and respond to them, we are thereby invited to ponder God's questions, challenges, and call in our lives. We are reminded that we are God's beloved children, and we are called to live out our discipleship to Jesus, to "pay attention to the deepest thing we know" (Steere). In this roll call, we are prompted by God's presence and summoned to prioritize God's priorities, not just during this prayer itself, but also throughout everything that the day brings.

In the praises we give to God, there are implied questions for us. Are you there? Are you ready? Are you available? Are you willing to work for and promote God's reign and priorities?

Some of the most challenging Bible verses interrogate us, cutting us to the heart. In Genesis 3:9, God asks Adam: "Where are you?" In Genesis 4:9, Cain tries to evade responsibility by answering God's question with one of his own: "Am I my brother's keeper?" In John 21:15 and following, Jesus asks Peter three times: "Do you love me?" God's challenge to Isaiah also confronts us: "Whom shall I send, and who will go for us?" (6:8). And in Matthew 16:15 Jesus asks his disciples a question that all of us face: "Who do you say that I am?"

Such questions are there every time we pray and celebrate liturgy of the hour traditions. In many versions of morning prayer, we hear the psalmist's refrain (in 95:7b-8):

> O that today you would listen to [God's] voice.
> Do not harden your hearts, as at Meribah,
> as on the day at Massah in the wilderness.

This is both a challenge and an invitation. We sometimes think that prayer is about influencing God, possibly by our petitions, perhaps by our piety. But here we see that prayer affects, influences, alters, and even altars us.

Some churches still do have a practice of sounding a bell several times a day. When I walked a month-long pilgrimage in Spain, no matter how far out in the countryside I might have been, I frequently heard bells, either regular resonant ringing from church towers or the erratic tin clatter from around the necks of grazing cows and sheep. Regardless of the source, I recognized that these peals were all a call and reminder to pray and claim my identity and role before God.

Bell ringing is an old church custom with several variations. We noted above that George Herbert observed it during morning and evening prayers. Elsewhere the practice is connected to the Angelus, an old medieval tradition created so that regular working folk who could not go to the church's elaborate services during the day could at least experience a small Office in the midst of their regular life. When neighbors heard such sounds, they were invited to stop work or whatever they happened to be doing and to remember prayerfully the angel's words to Mary (Luke 2:26-38). The famous Jean François Millet painting of peasants praying in a field (*The Angelus*, 1857–59), with a church in the background, beautifully illustrates this form of devotion. One monk sees the Angelus as a vital question, a role call,

> a daily opportunity . . . to consent to God's gift of [God's self] to me, and to say, "Here I am, Lord. . . . I am ready." Repeating Mary's words of acceptance becomes my act of yielding to God's will for me in the present situation. Day after day this custom places me before God in an attitude of total personal surrender.[13]

In such moments of praise and prayer, we too are invited to respond as did Isaiah to the Lord: "Here am I; send me" (6:8). Or as Mary (whose canticle is recited in evening prayer) to the angel Gabriel: "Here am I, the servant of the Lord; let it be with me according to your word" (Luke 1:38). Or as Peter to Jesus: "You are the Messiah, the Son of the living God" (Matthew 16:16).

Restoring the Missing Link

Often we forget and overlook that throughout our history Christians have offered worship to God in three ways: public worship, common prayer, and free private prayer. The Office is actually a missing link between corporate and personal prayer. Its absence, I suspect, has led to much confusion for Christians in both Sunday worship and personal prayer. Sunday worship is now sometimes distorted to meet felt consumer needs, therapeutic itches, or entertainment expectations. Private prayer can be twisted into narcissism. We all need a threefold worship and prayer life. The schism between corporate worship and private prayer could be healed if Christians practiced all three forms of prayer.

Praying together at a similar time (even when separated geographically) can profoundly reverse unhealthy individualism in our prayer. Moreover, honoring all three prayer forms actually means that they are united. Our lives—and the various kinds of prayers, on Sundays and during the week—weave themselves into one integrated whole.

As we grow in the practice of common prayer and devotions, our appreciation for corporate worship is reinforced. There are several ways that the Office connects to weekly communal praise, drawing from that worship but also deepening it.

On a continuum from corporate worship to private prayer, fixed-hour prayer falls in the middle. On one end Sunday worship involves a large group, less participation and contribution from every member, and much formality. Morning and evening prayer involves smaller groups and is more dependent on voluntary initiative and participation. Though it has a degree of formality, there is also more room for individual responses, petitions, and modifications. On the other end, private extemporaneous prayer is individual, informal, subjective, and relies on one's own initiative; in it one's offerings and utterances are individual.

Both Sunday worship and fixed-hour prayer follow the same basic threefold structure: praise (Psalms, hymns, canticles), listening to God (Scriptures, silence, homily), and responding to God (meditation, prayer, intercessions, commitments, offerings, praise, service, and ministry). Common prayer reiterates themes from Sunday worship and prepares us to sing God's praises with the larger group, recalling last week's service and helping us anticipate next week's. The Office is enhanced if what is sung there connects with what is sung on Sunday. People often say that they are better prepared for Sunday worship and more receptive to it when they regularly practice morning and evening prayer. As one congregant told me when I was teaching about the Office in our congregation, her practice of common prayer meant that "Sunday worship seems less out of sync with the rest of life."

The Office is a recommitment of primary values that we hear preached and that we proclaim each Sunday. It deepens and reinforces baptismal vows. That is one reason why many find it appropriate to recite great creeds as part of morning and evening prayer.

Like Sunday worship, common prayer is meant to be prayed with others. Ideally it should be offered, hosted, and encouraged by local groups or churches.

Thus even when one does have to pray it alone, one can remember the wider group of believers who are praying and, in a small but telling way, experience the communion of saints as well.

Another connection between Sunday worship and daily prayer is that for many centuries, as we saw above, churches rang bells several times a day to call people to pray. Those lovely invitations to prayer were an audible reminder from the very place and location where believers corporately worshipped.

Morning and evening prayer also connects with Sunday worship because certain elements (Psalms, Scriptures, responses, intercessions, petitions) change with the liturgical season. The daily routines and rhythms of prayer can help reinforce and deepen awareness of the church year.

Thus liturgy-of-the-hours disciplines offer much hope and promise in restoring the missing link between personal prayer and corporate worship. Even so, it can be an uphill battle to persuade people about the gifts of common prayer.

One particular obstacle in our day is contemporary resistance to and suspicion of disciplines and formality, especially in the spiritual life. Since we put so much emphasis on spontaneous inner experience and personal satisfaction, it is hard to believe that formal prayers can be worthwhile.

Are there other ways of understanding and looking at disciplines that can help us appreciate such prayer practices?

CHAPTER 6

The Freedom of Disciplines
The Primary Paradox of Prayer

When I go to the Middle East, I am impressed every day by the periodic ceasing of regular activity while prayers are publicly broadcast over outdoor loudspeakers. Muslims stop, spread rugs, kneel, and pray. Such prayers are not always convenient. My first night in Syria followed two long flights, an arrival around 2:00 a.m., and losing a previous night's sleep. It was not a pleasant surprise to be awakened by loud devotions within only a few hours of my arrival. Nevertheless, even while the prayers disoriented me, I recognized their worshipful quality, and that did leave me both challenged and encouraged.

In the West, Muslim minarets and their accompanying prayers are getting more familiar. In Oslo, Norway, Muslims were granted permission to broadcast prayers from rooftops once on Fridays (their holy day). Until then, the only legal call to prayer was the ringing of church bells. (The Norwegian Heathen Society was upset by this development and applied for and received permission for regular announcements of their meetings and values.)[1] Meanwhile, more recently in Switzerland, voters decided that Muslim immigrants were not allowed to construct minarets. Here in North America, I've seen Muslims say their prayers in airport lounges, jet aisles, and shopping malls.

I was once told of some Protestant pastors visiting the Holy Land for the first time. They were offended by Muslim prayers. "Lo, how the heathen rage," scoffed one. Yet praying regularly does not strike me as particularly heathen. We North American Christians seem far more heathen in our inability—or is that refusal?—to pray regularly. Ironically, there is a strong possibility that Muhammad learned his practice of regular daily prayers from a Christian hermit. If so, Muslims are more faithful than many Protestants in maintaining an ancient Christian tradition of morning and evening prayer. When a group of French Trappists decided to live out a witness to God's reconciling power in Algeria, a Muslim country largely hostile to all things French or Christian, their commitment to regular daily prayer was one of the important ways they demonstrated their serious faithfulness to their neighbors.[2]

John Moschos, a sixth-century monk, traveled through the Eastern Byzantine Christian world. One commentator observes: "Certainly if John Moschos were to come back today, it is likely that he would find much more that was familiar in the practices of a modern Muslim Sufi than he would with those of, say, a contemporary American Evangelical."[3] Ouch!

For many Christians, with our Western bias against the East and pejorative caricatures of Muslims, the challenging example of Islam will hardly be a compelling argument to take daily prayers seriously. More's the pity. We could learn a lot from others about the worth and value of recovering our own ancient and venerable Christian tradition.

Is God Not Everywhere and All the Time . . . and Always the Same?

When I teach about morning and evening prayer, I run into some common objections. People say that they can pray anywhere, at anytime, for after all God is everywhere and always available. They remind me of people who used to tell me—when they learned that I was a pastor—that they do not go to church on Sundays but prefer to worship God in the woods or on the golf course.

Yes, it is certainly true that God is everywhere and available to us at all times, but this does not rule out the importance of setting aside specific and particular moments and places for the worship of God. Benedict of Nursia also declared that God is present everywhere and then added, intriguingly: "But beyond the least doubt we should believe this to be especially true when we celebrate the divine office."[4]

A tale is told of a little Jewish lad who insisted on running off to the woods every single day, even though such behavior was strictly forbidden by his family. His parents were baffled by his rebellious pattern because in all other respects he was devout and obedient. Finally they turned in desperation to their rabbi for help. Could he persuade the young fellow to behave? The good teacher talked with the boy, explaining why he must not go into the trees anymore. The boy listened attentively to his teacher, but the next day he headed once again into the nearby forest. So the rabbi followed from a distance and witnessed the little one piously reciting the Shema among the trees, "Hear, O Israel: The Lord is our God, the Lord alone."

Afterward the rabbi asked him, "Why do you do this? Why do you go to the woods to pray? Is not God everywhere and always the same?"

Without hesitation, the little fellow responded: "Yes, that is true. God is everywhere and always the same. But I am not."

Since most of us are not everywhere and always the same, we need special times and places to draw our attention to God again. This then can inform, form, shape, inspire, and orient the rest of our lives (with the hope that we will grow more consistent, authentic, and integrated). Then we are better equipped to live with the truth and reality of God's ongoing presence everywhere and in all times.

Although some people are able to be always and everywhere attentive to God, most of us need more structure than that. I found, both in my own experience and in working with congregants and seminary students over the years, that prayer goes better when there are regular times to pray and even when there are particular locations for prayer.

When I drive into the parking lot of the monastery where I have been praying, worshipping, and retreating for three decades, I can feel the tension automatically draining off my shoulders. My body knows how to pray there and knows what to expect when I am there. (This is all the more remarkable since I am not usually attuned to my body.)

Mennonites are, with good reason, sometimes leery of believing that certain places can lead us into being prayerful. So there has long been a custom of keeping buildings plain and not too fancy. Ironically, the simplicity of many of those structures is itself a particular aesthetic, one that invites a sense of adoration and even quiet awe. But ambivalence about buildings backfires too. A pastor once asked me how he could make Sunday mornings more worshipful when the door to the bathroom was at the front of the sanctuary, near the pulpit: the whole congregation could see whenever anyone went in and came out. Thinking about what's taking someone so long in there could very well distract from focusing on worship.

Some Mennonite edifices are rather plain and not even called "churches" but instead "meetinghouses." What many do not realize is that the original sense of "meetinghouse" was not just about meeting other people but especially about meeting God in and through worship. The book of Exodus, for example, speaks of the tent of meeting:

> At the entrance of the tent of meeting before the
> Lord, . . . I will meet with you, to speak to you
> there. I will meet with the Israelites there, and
> it shall be sanctified to my glory; I will conse-
> crate the tent of meeting and the altar. (Exodus
> 29:42b-44a)

Formal spaces can and do affect our spiritual life.
As a pastor, I was intrigued about how even though
we insisted that "church" is the people and not the
structure, and even though we called that structure
a "church *building*," many people behaved differently when they entered the door. Their voices low-
ered, or they began humming hymns, even if they
were stopping by in the middle of the week.

When I went to attend Associated Mennonite
Biblical Seminary as a young adult, I was pleased
to learn ahead of time that its chapel featured a
prayer room. I planned in advance to go there
often. But I tried to pray in that room one or
two times and was unable to so. The cold, dark
red, brick walls loomed high, with little natural
light. The seats were uncomfortable. One rumor
suggested that the prayer room was supposed
to remind us of cells in which sixteenth-century
Anabaptists were imprisoned. I noticed that not
many other people prayed there either. The room
was often used for storage, as a large closet. Why
not? Space is not sacred, few people prayed there,
and Mennonites like to be practical.

After I returned as a professor two decades later,

however, the school received a generous donation for a relatively small place that was named the Chapel of the Word. It was carefully designed, with attention to space and pleasing light. There are big windows, curved walls, and an abundance of wood. Although it had many purposes (since Mennonites after all are practical), including teaching and practicing various worship arts, it soon became a regular place of campus prayer. Different clusters of folks met there to pray several times a week, week after week, including those who prayed with various versions of *Take Our Moments and Our Days*. Yes, God is everywhere and always the same. But we are not. We need to cultivate our receptivity to God's initiative and grace.

The Primary Paradox of Prayer: Grace and Discipline

Prayer—as part of our relationship with God— is a gift. God starts and initiates it, whether we deserve it or not, ask for it or not, pay attention to it or not. At first in the book of Exodus there is no indication that Moses was looking for, waiting for, longing for, or even particularly interested in God. We do not know whether he was especially observant or faithful. We do know that he was an escaped criminal, a fugitive, a murderer who abandoned his own people and the people who had adopted him. Yet God chose and called him. God took the initiative with Moses as God does with us as well.

But then we are invited to respond. Prayer is one way that we accept God's gracious move toward us and indicate our availability to God. We cannot finally "keep company with God" (Clement of Alexandria's description of prayer[5]) and grow with God unless we respond to God's initiative. Like Moses in Exodus 3:3-4, we too must "turn aside and look at this great sight," and when God addresses us, we also must say, "Here I am." Though a life of prayer is grace-filled, it also depends on our response of discipline and, yes, even work.

As I explained earlier, my bird-watching began without deliberation. I went for regular walks in a nearby park. One day a friend lent me a zoom lens, and I was astounded by what I saw. Discovering birds was an accident of grace. They were there all along, just as they had been in my childhood neighborhood all along, but I had never noticed anything besides the LBJs, Little Brown Jobs.

But bird-watching is not just or only grace: it is also discipline. After unexpectedly encountering marvelous sightings one afternoon in the riverside park, I decided to watch birds more carefully and to learn more about them. This entailed the acquiring of tools: binoculars and a field guide were useful. Learning involves practice, the acquisition of skills. I had to go where birds would likely be found. Once there, I needed to be quiet and wait, sometimes for a long, long while. Much of this is like the life and discipline of prayer.

Yet disciplines guarantee nothing. You may have

pricey binoculars and the most up-to-date field guide and go to likely bird venues—the woods, marsh, or shore—and still see nothing astounding. You might not observe a single bird, let alone an interesting one. But the chances are always better with disciplines in place. Prayer is like that: discipline is no guarantee that we will encounter God, but our chances improve.

Seeing birds is always paradoxical. There are no guarantees, although discipline often helps. When I visited Costa Rica, I was excited because that is one of the world's best places for bird-watching. My friend Mark Chupp (who was then serving with Mennonite Central Committee) and I went to a famous rain forest, both hoping to see a rare and lovely emerald green quetzal. We knew that some people went to that area for days at a time without ever sighting one of those stunning creatures. We were there for twenty-four hours and saw a quetzal three or four times. Partly it was the discipline of being in the right place at the right time and knowing how and where to look and listen. But partly it was also grace and good fortune. We certainly did not "deserve" such a sighting.

Sometimes birding happens by grace, even by accident. I have seen good birds as I drove along a busy road, a snowy owl and snow buntings, though not looking for them. Once I saw an anhinga, of all things, in a small Michigan lake, even though it was much farther north than usual. Another time a wild turkey wandered into our suburban backyard. Boy, was he lost!

But even so, discipline was involved in such moments of grace. That is because one cannot see what one does not notice. And one does not notice if one is not paying attention. I would not have recognized the birds on the road, in that lake, or in my backyard if I had not developed bird-watching disciplines. Like Moses, we all must learn how to "turn aside and look at this great sight."

God's grace is all around and often abundantly available to us, but we seldom notice or know it. A nineteenth-century poem by Elizabeth Barrett Browning sums this up well:

> Earth's crammed with heaven,
> And every common bush afire with God;
> But only he who sees, takes off his shoes.
> The rest sit round it, and pluck blackberries,
> And daub their natural faces unaware.[6]

And that's why disciplines are essential.

Holy Habits

We sometimes connect discipline with another unappreciated and despised word: "habit." We associate this term with "empty habits" or—far worse—"bad habits" or even "nasty habits." Though habits, like disciplines, can certainly be meaningless, empty, or nasty, they do not have to be so. Habits also have a potential for being positive and rich.

As a pastor, every week I encouraged my congregation to share things for which we were grateful. We did this as part of the offering time in our worship. After each named gift, the entire congregation would respond, "Thanks be to God," preferably with vigor and enthusiasm.

One summer day our family came home from an all-day outing. When we got back, my wife discovered that we had not turned off a stove burner before we left. As if this were not bad enough, she also saw that we had left a cloth oven mitt near that live burner. It could easily have caught fire and ignited a costly conflagration. Fortunately, it had been treated with some flame retardant, and no harm was done, other than blackening an edge of the mitt.

My wife showed this to our son, who was then eleven, and she said, "All I can say is 'Thanks be to God.'"

"I already did," he responded.

There a regularly practiced habit bore fruit. A learned refrain from Sunday morning worship informed Lorna and Paul's lives and their attitudes, and even their reading and interpretation of their circumstances.

Similarly, a common-hour prayer habit teaches us words and refrains that help us understand, interpret, and frame whatever happens in our lives:

> Glory to the Father, and to the Son, and to the Holy Spirit,
> as it was in the beginning, is now, and will be forever. Amen.

O God, make speed to save us;
O Lord, make haste to help us.

O Lord, open our lips;
and our mouth shall declare your praise.[7]

Lines from *Take Our Moments and Our Days* are equally rich:

You are good to those who wait for you,
to all who seek you.

My heart is ready, O God:
I will sing your praise.

Be exalted, O God, above the heavens,
and let your glory shine over all the earth.

We declare your steadfast love in the morning,
and your faithfulness by night.

There is no day where such holy phrases are irrelevant. Habits of prayer can help make them an intrinsic part of our lives.

The Paradoxical Freedom of Discipline

We often think of discipline as restrictive or limiting, especially in spirituality. But Richard Foster, an evangelical Quaker and an influential contemporary writer on prayer, has a different understanding. He contends that such an approach actually has to do with freedom, appropriateness, and discernment. A person of discipline

> can do what needs to be done when it needs to be done. The disciplined person is the person who can live in the appropriateness of the hour. The extreme ascetic and the glutton have exactly the same problem: they cannot live appropriately; they cannot do what needs to be done when it needs to be done.[8]

A disciplined person understands the "signs of the times" and acts appropriately, being free to do what is necessary in the moment.

Tales from the Desert Fathers and Mothers often deal with paradoxes of asceticism versus grace, joy, and hospitality. This story is about Anthony, an important desert Christian (second and third century):

> A hunter in the desert saw Abba Anthony enjoying himself with the brethren and he was shocked. Wanting to show [the hunter] that it was necessary sometimes to meet the needs of the brethren, the old man said to him, "Put an arrow in your bow and shoot it." So he did. The old man then said, "Shoot another," and he did so. Then the old man said, "Shoot yet again," and the hunter replied, "If I bend my bow so much I will break it." Then the old man said to him, "It is the same with the work of God. If we stretch the brethren beyond measure, they will soon break.

Sometimes it is necessary to come down to meet their needs." When he heard these words, the hunter was pierced by compunction, and greatly edified by the old man, he went away. As for the brethren, they went home strengthened.[9]

Anthony was free to do the right thing at the appropriate moment. Sometimes it's time to pray; sometimes it's time to party. Anthony's freedom was learned because he was a man of tremendous and faithful discipline.

Discipline is the liberty to perform beyond prior limitations. It is neither total restriction nor absolute license. Rather, it helps us understand and do what is proper when needed; it develops our responses and reactions, enabling us to live according to our priorities. It helps our character to grow, develop, and mature.

We know that our muscles have memory, which is nurtured and built up through practice and repetition. When I was learning to windsurf, I fell into the water a lot. Whether it was due to bug bites, boat wakes, wind shifts, muscle spasms, lack of attention, or poor balance, it did not take much to dunk me once again. (In the first congregation that I used to pastor, we sprinkled folks in the pews with water on Pentecost and called out: "Remember your baptism and be thankful." Learning to windsurf often gave me opportunity to recall my baptism by immersion.) But I'll never forget the surprise when one day I went to the lake, got on my board, sailed across the water with no trouble, and sailed right back again. Yet I had difficulty telling my friends precisely how to do this. How could I explain something that had never happened before? My body had learned things through practice; my muscles knew what to do, even if I could not articulate how. In the same way, our hearts, minds, and souls are conditioned for faithfulness through the deliberate, and even at times, repetitive disciplines of prayer.

More than that, some things become easier as one masters a discipline. When I began windsurfing, one of the hardest jobs was lifting the mast and sail out of the water while standing and balancing on the surfboard. As a beginner, I often dropped the mast while sailing and thus repeatedly had to raise it. But as I practiced more and more, my arms, legs, and back grew stronger for the lifting; ironically, I also hardly ever dropped the mast, so I did not need to pull it up as often. Because discipline improved my performance, everything was easier.

Chickadees and Disciplines of Grace

Many years ago, on a cold winter day, our daughter, Erin (then age ten), came home quite excited. Her class had gone on a field trip to a nearby nature reserve. There they had learned to feed wild chickadees by hand.

She told us that no fewer than twenty-nine chickadees sat on and ate from her palm that day. Our daughter is a lifelong nature lover and was euphoric with this experience. We were all in awe of what she told us, not having experienced anything similar ourselves. We talked to her about Francis of Assisi and his ability to relate to wild animals.

With evangelistic zeal, Erin did not rest content until we too experienced this wonder. She began an impressive lobbying campaign to get us to go soon to the nature reserve. We all agreed without too much persuasion.

The designated day for our trip was bitterly cold, one of the iciest of an especially fierce winter. Even before we left, and again in the car, Erin began offering advice and tips on the art—or discipline—of feeding chickadees from one's hand: how to hold one's arm and palm, remaining perfectly still, standing near trees, making certain noises, not fearing or being startled by the little creatures, and not worrying about whether their claws would hurt. As Erin's excitement mounted, so did ours.

Carrying our bag of seeds, we made our way across a field, fighting the fierce wind, and came to a sheltered grove. We found places among the trees, assumed the posture Erin recommended, and acted like statues with palms upturned, waiting for grace.

All was peaceful. We heard the wind, but here it did not cut us so sharply. The trees were snow-laden and lovely. We could see or hear no one else. Gradually, chickadees came near, and even more slowly they took the plunge of visiting our uplifted palms, floating onto our hands as delicately as drifting snowflakes.

When one hopped onto my hand, I hardly dared to breathe. It was so tiny and fragile that I could not even feel its weight. (Because of the cold I was not barehanded, alas.) I marveled at how vulnerable the little creature was and wondered at its intricate beauty.

After we had all been visited many times by the small birds, we reluctantly gave in to the cold and trudged away. We all agreed that the words "magical" and even "miraculous" were not over-stated. It was a moment of holy, contemplative silence such as one seldom experiences.

It was fully possible that we could have stood in that grove for hours rather than twenty minutes and not have one chickadee approach us. We might have seen the value and worth of our time there as completely dependent on how "successful" or "efficient" we were. If no birds came, we could have stomped away in disgust and disillusion. But that would be to miss the point.

Our time in the woods was one of holy availability. We were open to whatever might happen or appear. We could do the right disciplines—as Erin carefully instructed us—but none of us could guarantee the outcome. In the same way, when we pray, we open ourselves to God but do not demand that God make us fruitful, effective, or better.

This time in the woods was an experience of communion with ourselves, with each other, with nature, and with God. We were all awed by it. We drank in the beauty and marveled at it. In the same way, prayer is an opportunity for deeper communion.

Ultimately, our prayers and disciplines are not for any purpose except that of deepening our relationship with God and increasing our availability to God—the relationship that is at the heart of our lives' meaning and that transforms all our other relationships too.

Discipline, then, frees and enriches us in many significant ways. Nevertheless, the particular discipline of common prayer can offer other challenges and difficulties.

CHAPTER 7

Wrestling for a Blessing
Challenges of Morning and Evening Prayer

john Howard Griffin is famous for his classic book *Black Like Me,* which helped expose the horrors and ugliness of racism. As a white man, he darkened his skin with dyes and chemicals to experience in a small way what others endured nonstop in Jim Crow culture in the South, where he lived. His book received acclaim, but many hated him and threatened him at times with death, even in his own hometown. In spite of his fame, a good number of people do not know that Griffin was motivated for such risky action by his deep Christian faith. Much else about this remarkable man is also overlooked.

While Griffin was serving in the military in the South Pacific during World War II, an explosion totally blinded him. He nevertheless managed to go on and accomplish many things, including writing two novels, marrying, and raising children. Then in the late 1950s, something miraculous happened. His sight unexpectedly returned: no one is quite sure why. For the first time he was able to see his wife and children. Most of us can hardly imagine how precious that must have been.

One of the greatest gifts of this reprieve—in his words, the "full reason and justification for seeing again"—was the fact that he was able to pray the divine hours once more. He called such common prayer "the soul's nourishment, the soul's normalcy, sinking beyond the words to their innermost meaning, seeking and thirsting for it."[1]

My guess is that most of us would not regard the ability to pray the liturgy of the hours as a primary benefit of recovering one's sight. And his assertion is all the more remarkable since Griffin used a lengthy pre-Vatican II prayer book that was unwieldy and impractical for most laypersons.

The challenges of praying the Office today are in no way comparable to the difficulties that Griffin faced. Nevertheless this is no easy practice. And we must frankly examine the barriers.

I once visited a novice monk whose primary work was in the infirmary, caring for the sick. He said he loved his annual weeklong hermitage retreat because then he did "not have to go to the Office." I was confused because he had no desk job. What did he mean? He was referring to the monastery's daily worship schedule, a demanding form of prayer that was challenging: too much for him, as it turns out. Perhaps it was no surprise that although there was much that he loved about monastic life, he did not complete his novitiate.

The spiritual life is not always easy. That is one reason why I love the image of wrestling for a blessing. Jacob faced an unknown foe in his nighttime struggle. He received a paradoxical blessing and in the process was also wounded (Genesis 33). Common prayer is not necessarily easy, yet we may fully expect that even and perhaps especially there, God can touch and bless us. Still, it will not automatically mean smooth sailing. Sometimes daily prayer can feel like a grueling wrestling match; we might end up with a limp afterward.

But Is It Personally Meaningful?

From time to time, people tell me that they would pray the hours only if doing so were "personally meaningful" at a particular time in their life. While I know such prayer is not for everyone, this subjective approach nevertheless troubles me.

This attitude plays into the individualism of so much personal spirituality, especially since the Reformation. Although Christians are called to be community oriented—"For where two or three are gathered in my name, I am there among them" (Matthew 18:20)—many of us are more and more afflicted by isolation and disconnection.

Should we be willing to do things that do not feel personally meaningful if we know them to be good for the body of Christ? When I worked with a church group (an experiment I describe in a later chapter) to pray morning and evening prayers during the Easter season, it was striking that this common practice was so helpful to some, including ones who had not prayed for a long time, if ever. Several group members had never been able to maintain a prayer discipline for one week, let alone an entire church season. One participant with a strong, self-directed devotional life talked with us about how hard this prayer was. We asked whether it helped to see her participation as supporting "weaker" members. This did make sense to her. The "strong" might take on certain disciplines for the sake of upholding and encouraging the "weak."

I also question whether we always know what we most need and whether that need always seems meaningful. I do not feel like flossing my teeth every day; actually, I almost never feel like flossing my teeth. And my high dentist bills and costly root canals over the years prove that. When my children were small, I did not always feel like changing their diapers. I do not always feel like listening to people who are sad or angry. When I worked on university and seminary degrees, the various requirements did not always feel "personally meaningful." What does this phrase mean? Does it have to feel good to us before we do it?

At times we may come to be overly dependent on emotions. Dietrich Bonhoeffer warned against prayer being "governed by moods which have nothing to do with the spiritual life."[2] Feelings go through many transitions. We may not know how to pray (or feel like praying) when we do not sense God's presence. Yet the divine hours provide regularity and constancy in prayer, regardless of the vagaries of our emotions.

Praying neither "comes naturally" nor makes intuitive sense. Stanley Hauerwas and William Willimon have argued that in the Christian walk "our lives are bent toward God in a way that is not of our natural inclination." This is important, they write, "in a society that worships individual autonomy, freedom, and detachment, a culture that has taught us to live so that we are determined by no tradition, [so] that we are accountable to nothing outside the self." We must, they say, question whether "personal choice is the highest human virtue."[3] Praying according to feeling or inclination "is more to seek consolation than to risk conversion. To pray only when it suits us is to want God on our terms," says Joan Chittister.[4]

Spiritual disciplines ultimately are not so much about what feels "personally meaningful" but more about repentance and conversion. Too often our preferred prayer does not pay attention to God but to our own concerns, needs, and priorities. Praying means moving beyond what is merely personally meaningful now and allowing our agenda to be shaped by something—or better, Someone—beyond us.

The Noise of My Enemy

One summer week I was struggling with being let down by a friend. In the midst of those tumultuous feelings, on a particularly lovely day, I decided to do my devotions outside. I found a private corner in my backyard to pray. To my surprise, I realized that the very friend who preoccupied me was working on a roof down the block. If he had peeked over the fence, he could have seen me praying in my lawn chair. I tried to put him out of my mind, but that was not easily done.

That day's readings happened to call for Psalm 55. I immediately resonated with it: "I am distraught by the *noise* of the enemy" (vv. 2-3). I could literally hear my friend's hammering a few doors down.

> It is not enemies who taunt me—
>   I could bear that;
> it is not adversaries who deal insolently with me—
>   I could hide from them.
> But it is you, my equal,
>   my companion, my familiar friend. (vv. 12-14)

I could relate. Often in the midst of prayer I start to surface and recognize my resentments of others and even my vengeful thoughts.

As I continued with the psalm, two phrases caught me: "But I call upon God, and the Lord will save me" and "Cast your burden on the Lord, and [God] will sustain you" (vv. 16, 22). This reminded me to trust in and rely on God even when I find others, including friends, unreliable.

When I had finished praying, I knew what was required. I walked down the block to see my friend and said, "We need to talk." That was the first step toward our reconciliation.

If I had chosen a psalm I wanted to pray that

day, a psalm that suited my particular mood of being betrayed, it would not have been Psalm 55. That psalm might not have seemed personally fulfilling to me at the time. But that prayer converted me and led to a healed friendship. Choosing to pray "imposed" prayers is often called praying objectively because we do it regardless of personal feelings and preferences.

Challenges of Repetition

One objection to fixed-hour prayer is repetition. Many people today resent sameness, whether in daily prayers or Sunday worship, and long for things to be innovative and always new. But repetition also has its virtues. It gives us an accumulated store of knowledge upon which to draw, preparing us to receive unprecedented insights. Often as I walk, phrases surface that I have sung in church settings long before, and I find myself singing, even though I have never put any deliberate work into memorizing sacred songs. Repetition accomplishes that.

We are not always ready or able to hear a particular Scripture. But if we repeatedly ponder Bible texts, memorize them, and learn them by "heart," they can be near and deep, form our lives, and speak to us when we need to receive them. As children, all of my peers and I were the offspring of folks who had lived through World War II. We knew people who had even survived concentration camps. And we often heard stories of how Bible texts that people knew by heart had sustained them through those dire difficulties. Prisoners, we were told, gathered huge swaths of texts that they knew, compiling makeshift Bibles. They were grateful for whatever they had memorized.

It is important to do such vital preparatory work in an ongoing way so that when there are times of crisis, the texts and their meanings will be available to us and we can draw upon them. In putting together *Take Our Moments and Our Days*, we editors often spoke of how repeated use of short Scripture passages in the services would help people memorize key Bible verses.

Repetition can actually convince and convert us. Hearing something once may not be enough for us to take in, learn, or understand. That is why advertisers are so repetitive. I have often heard the cliché that something needs to be presented seven times before people ever hear it. (Is that why many monks pray seven times a day?) Similar dynamics are at work in the spiritual life. This reminds me of another Desert Father insight:

> Abba Poemen said: The nature of water is yielding, and that of a stone is hard. Yet if you hang a bottle filled with water above the stone so that the water drips drop by drop, it will wear a hole in the stone. In the same way the word of God is tender, and our heart is hard. So when people hear the word of God frequently, their hearts are opened to the fear of God.[5]

We often resist the provocation of Scriptures, even when they are repeated. Understandably so when they challenge our deepest beliefs or stubborn and misguided priorities. There are things in the Bible that we do not catch, understand, or absorb during one or two readings. We need to hear them again and again. Perhaps part of us resents repetition because it forces us to plumb deeper. We may dislike hearing over and over again words that unsettle us and make us uncomfortable. Thus David Adam told me in my interview with him:

> It's a bit like turning a drill. It might appear boring, but the more you are turning, the deeper you get. It's literally boring. But if you only turn it once, you don't get very far.

Common prayer immerses us in Scriptures. Repetition potentially deepens the meaning of such texts and helps us to live and understand them more fully.

Once, Henri Nouwen guided me on a retreat for five days. His method was simple. Each morning he gave me a familiar Gospel text—the annunciation to Mary, Zechariah's canticle, and so forth—and asked me to ponder that all day long and then to speak to him about the passage at the end of the day. I knew all the selections well, having often heard and read and studied them over the years. But I dutifully sat with them, reading and repeating them over and again for an hour at a time. And

I saw things in each text that I had never noticed before. Some of the verses still speak freshly to me now, some fifteen years later, on the basis of things I discovered at that simple retreat. Such are the merits and benefits of repetition.

Yielding to God in Worship

Common morning and evening hours can be a difficult form of prayer. Perhaps this should not surprise us since even the term "Office" itself carries the suggestion of responsibility, duty, and burden.

One helpful way of praying such a challenging practice is to yield to it. My temptation is to take in and analyze every word: but there is too much to absorb each time. I need to be immersed in it again and again, to be carried along and away with words given us by God.

Sometimes I visit a Coptic Orthodox church for Sunday worship. There are many things that I love about being there. The three-hour liturgy astounds me and—even more astonishing—a good part of that service every week is almost identical. Some Scriptures and the short sermon change, but many of the same prayers and hymns recur each week. Obviously my Coptic friends do not suffer from the Western malady of a low boredom threshold.

As I worship there, listening to the music, smelling incense, hearing many prayers in languages that I do not necessarily understand, something often happens within. At some point during the service, I surrender to the movement of the worship. *I believe,*

I cry out in my heart. I allow myself to be carried along on the waves of that service. Similar things occur in charismatic worship or in other traditions such as African-American churches that do not pay much attention to the clock while worshipping.

Fixed-hour prayer functions this way, too. It works on us time after time, again and again, sweeping us into worship and carrying us into God's purposes, if we will only yield. This can never happen if we cling to skeptical "been there, done that" attitudes about the spiritual life and its practices.

Finding God in the Boring Ordinary

Often we expect to be entertained in worship. This demand for amusement is a factor in so-called worship-war controversies. Let's face it, however: wanting to be perpetually diverted is immature. Children's complaints of being "bored" often have to do with their own learned or acquired limitations. When they were small, they had no trouble being fascinated in all manner of circumstances.

Yes, it is true that some duties and responsibilities do feel boring at times. Much of life consists of repeating the same things day after day. They are ordinary and repetitive, but also necessary and vital. And many of them are very, very good, even the best things in life: saying "thank you" for good deeds done, feeding those we love, extending hospitality to neighbors, taking care of one's body. This is also an important aspect of the Office. It assists us to see the holy in the mundane.

Meeting God or at least waiting for God amid boredom helps us realize the holy in the common and routine. Just as God is available even in the repetition of disciplined prayer, so God is present in life's humdrums. God is not only manifest in the ecstatic, spectacular, exceptional, or extraordinary. All time is sacred: hence we employ the term "sanctification of time."

Spiritual masters invariably tell us that no matter how well or how euphoric our prayer goes for a time, especially in the early days, sooner or later we "hit a wall." Whether it is "desolation" or "dark night," the solution is not to give up on prayer at that point and then try something else. Rather, spiritual growth requires one to endure and move through that particular wilderness. Showing up and hanging in there are important. The *Rule of Taizé* acknowledges that sometimes faithful common prayer observance not only is not heartfelt but also is downright difficult: "There will be days when the Office is a burden to you. On such occasions know how to offer your body, since your presence itself already signifies your desire, momentarily unrealizable, to praise your Lord."[6] Simple persistent faithfulness is important, even vital. Brother Émile of Taizé told me:

> No matter how beautiful a prayer is, there's always going to be a need for perseverance, for commitment, and for being faithful. There will be times when we don't feel the beauty. Then we pray the question rather than what we feel.

The hope certainly is that one does eventually move beyond the rote, automatic, or mechanical. But this may be possible only after facing one's problems and limitations in a self-awareness that emerges in and through and beyond boredom. In other words, boredom might be important for self-knowledge. Once when I was complaining about a situation in my life, a wise guide counseled me, "Go deeper." My urge was to flee, to move on, to go elsewhere. But this person helped me see that the problem of boredom was not with just my own external circumstances but also with how I functioned in them. The uncomfortable situation was calling for my growth. While I wanted to alter what was happening around me, I was the one who most needed to change.

Common prayer, as C. W. McPherson points out, is a long-term commitment that parallels:

> human experiences: an exclusive sexual relationship over a long time; practice of an art or a skill to mastery; raising a child or mentoring a young person. All these require a daily, or near daily, commitment. All involve periods of . . . monotony as well as occasional periods of disruptive challenge. All can eventuate in joy.[7]

Moving beyond Monotony

I am certainly not arguing for rote and boring prayer. Learning to pray the liturgy of the hours, with all its challenges, is meant to lead us into being prayerful, in the same way that practicing scales helps us learn to play musical instruments—savoring, enjoying, and being drawn into the music.

Though it often feels like the Office is "all the same," even so there is or can be much variety. Psalms and Scripture shift and change every day. Prayers, readings, and responses to Bible passages vary with church seasons, and some elements are new each week. If that is not enough variety, we also have choices to make within the prayers: how long to spend in silence, selecting hymns to sing, subjects for intercession. *Take Our Moments and Our Days* was never meant to be prayed woodenly or legalistically in its precise form. Pray-ers are invited to discern how they might shorten or even skip certain elements or perhaps add and expand other aspects, appropriately modifying the forms for their own contexts.

Offerings That Cost Us Nothing?
There is, I believe, at least one other major reason why we sometimes avoid or resist this intense discipline. Norman Shanks, leader of the Iona Community, spoke to me at length about his group's common prayer. Though there are many current cultural obstacles to such observance, the truth is that this kind of spiritual practice exposes us to the gospel and radically challenges us. Shanks said, "If one takes the actual words . . . seriously, some of it's quite hard. The God reflected is a God whose love is compassionate and steadfast but also is tough."

Christian faith is challenging. One of my friends— let's call her Julie—is an eloquent preacher and passionate pastor. She occasionally has congregants tell her that they are uneasy with her preaching on the cost of discipleship. They want a faith that is a little more casual, upbeat, and uplifting. They want to come to church on Sunday morning for comfort and pep talks. But the Bible too often calls us to act, be different, reevaluate how we live, change what we do. We need to hear provocative Scripture passages over and over again precisely because of our natural reluctance, which leads us to resist the very real costs of discipleship.

Our God does not let us off easily. We are drawn into following Jesus, the way of the cross, a demanding and tough route. That is why it is important that we not be in charge of selecting our Bible texts each day. It is too easy to choose ones that always comfort or console and consistently reinforce and agree with our point of view. Biblical faith requires us to be vulnerable to accountability, to repentance, and to a change of heart. This is absolutely essential if we are to grow in our faith.

I do not apologize for this difficulty. I agree with Gandhi, who apparently said that one major social sin is "worship without sacrifice." We cannot offer praise to God without being substantially altered and reworked ourselves.

Thus it is also no surprise that in their morning prayers the members of the Iona Community boldly declare: "We will not offer to God offerings that cost us nothing" (cf. 2 Samuel 24:24).

But paradoxically, such offerings also return great gifts to us.

CHAPTER 8

Giving at the Office

Blessings and Benefits of Morning and Evening Prayer

*n*elson Kraybill is an enthusiastic proponent of common morning and evening prayer, and over the years we often have compared notes about this way of praying. Some time ago this pastor, New Testament scholar, and author boarded a plane and politely engaged the stranger beside him in conversation. He told me the story this way: "I really took notice . . . when during the flight the young man pulled out the Roman Catholic liturgy of the hours. He explained that he was in seminary, preparing for the priesthood, and he invited me to join him for prayers.

"It seemed wise not to sing the hymns aloud in a cabin full of other travelers," Kraybill told me with a laugh, "but we read aloud the liturgy and spoke prayers of blessing for each other's ministry. At thirty thousand feet, two strangers recognized each other as brothers in Christ, sharing a journey. More than anything that happened in our exchange, it was that shared prayer that established common ground and bridged denominational differences between us."

This way of praying offers us many gifts. In

our culture, saying "I gave at the Office" is a way to avoid further commitment because we allegedly did our duty elsewhere. But faithful Office observance also gives to us. There are many benefits in such prayer.

This is not to suggest seeing this practice as a commodity, using it for what we can get from or out of it. But we do want to acknowledge and celebrate what it offers. Morning and evening prayer is not necessarily only an onerous or empty duty (although some have made it into one) but can be a tremendous opportunity.

My conviction is that the intrinsic benefits and purposes of such prayer far outweigh the difficulties and burdens that we have already examined.

The Gift of Words

The primary gift of the Office is quite simple: it provides words to pray. Not all would accept this. Some say that the best prayers are authentic only when they are spontaneous and extemporaneous. In this spirit, some complain when preachers or worship leaders use written texts. Richard Foster, an evangelical Quaker, tried to live without liturgy for a time and could not do so because "regular patterns . . . are, in fact, God-ordained means of grace." After all, he adds, "the Bible is full of rituals, liturgies, and ceremonies of all kinds."[1] We may value extemporaneous prayers over set prayers, yet God continues to speak and has spoken for years through the "fixed" language of Scriptures.

Furthermore, many do not have the words with which to approach God. They do not know how to pray, dare not pray, think their prayers are not worthy, or even have not a clue about what to say to God. Seminary students regularly report the following to me: "At church, they keep saying that I should pray and read my Bible. But no one explains *how*. They just say we have to do it." I suspect that my students are not the only believers with such struggles.

In my church I once gathered a group of people who committed themselves to morning and evening prayers for the Easter season. The very idea was new to most of them, and not one of them had taken on such a discipline before. Along the way several commented on how much they appreciated being given words to pray and ponder. Such prayer "covers it all efficiently," said one, and added, "I don't have to be worried that I've missed something." She no longer fretted about whether her prayer was sufficient, appropriate, or balanced. She discovered freedom and release. Another participant, suspicious of all things liturgical, told me: "I was surprised by how much I liked it. I didn't think I'd respond to someone else's words."

Foster, a Quaker and thus far from liturgical traditions, nevertheless argues that a given formula has many benefits. It "helps us articulate the yearnings of the heart that cry for expression" and sometimes will "prime the pump" for us to say more.

Liturgy brings us into unity and communion with other Christians who pray these prayers. Religious formulas resist "the temptation to be spectacular and entertaining." Formalized language reminds us that prayer calls us to engage the world on God's behalf and is not just privatized faith. It also

> helps us avoid the familiarity that breeds contempt. The intimacy of prayer must be always counterbalanced by the infinite distance of creature to Creator. In the Bible it is common for those who encounter God to fall on their face as though dead. The stateliness and formality of the liturgy help us realize that we are in the presence of real Royalty.[2]

While God is our friend and intimate companion, God is not our buddy or cozy companionable teddy bear. English is not always good at conveying awe and transcendence. In many languages—French, German, Dutch, or Spanish for example—one is careful about whom one addresses casually. Some people merit informal approaches; others deserve and rightly expect formal address. In prayer and worship, there is a case to be made for using beautiful and eloquent language while communicating with God.

Mark Galli, a *Christianity Today* editor, tells how hard it was for him previously as a pastor for ten years "to come up with fresh, creative, relevant prayers each week for worship. I found my compositions increasingly vapid." Much later he interviewed Kathleen Norris and came to new understandings. She was concerned about language that does not do justice to mystery. Church vocabulary, she said, should not be that of the market, media, workplace, or TV.

We could have good discussions about what it means to use culturally meaningful language, but Norris is also surely right in this:

> The church needs to give people "memorable speech" (as one poet put it). The Scriptures provide that royally. There's all sorts of memorable speech in the Psalms and the Gospels.[3]

The Gift of Words for Tough Times

Along the way I have shared how after my sister's death I lost the ability or desire to pray; at that time a Taizé prayer book helped me greatly. Many people have similar testimonies. An evangelical experienced a period of dryness during a serious depression but then found the *Book of Common Prayer*: "It was like being winched slowly out of a pit," he writes evocatively.[4]

In the Easter season prayer group in my former congregation, one person struggled for a long time with a terrible family tragedy: the untimely, unnecessary, self-inflicted death of a close relative. Several times she testified that it was our common prayer together that enabled her to pray for the first time in years.

Learned prayers—even rote prayers—can do this. A congregant once told me that when he was on the operating-room table, he was so afraid that he felt unable to pray . . . until he remembered the Lord's Prayer. A different church member had just had yet another discouraging visit with her young adult son; they never seemed to make progress in their relationship together. She was overcome with tears and unable to pray about it . . . until she recalled the words of confession that her congregation repeated every Sunday.

It is little surprise, then, that one version of the Office that I particularly like and recommend is *For Those We Love but See No Longer: Daily Offices for Times of Grief*, by Lisa Belcher Hamilton. She maintains that fixed and formal prayer, in the midst of grief, can do several things. It gives "a nourishing structure in difficult days and clears the way for a more honest knowledge of God, yourself, and your relationships with God and your loved one." It also "offers us a larger purpose than learning to live with our own pain."[5]

A good friend, Anna, began praying this way, using the *New Zealand Prayer Book* with her husband after he underwent surgery for a cancer that proved to be terminal within the year. Married for twenty-seven years, they had never practiced such a discipline before. It was important for how they spent their final months together, especially in giving thanks for each precious day. For years afterward Anna continued to pray with this book regularly and found "consolation in hard times and thankfulness in good times," she told me.

Morning and evening prayer is a gift in difficult phases and transitions, even when we have trouble with God and our relationship with God. As David Adam told me:

> If you come across a dry time in your life or a down time, you've actually got this resource [common prayer] . . . which you can call on, even if you may have to say it quite coolly. You can still say it. I compare it to my wife's cooking. Even when she's not that fond of me, she still cooks for me.

School of Prayer

A primary benefit of the Office is that it teaches us to pray. Some might object. Do we really *learn* to pray? Is prayer acquired in that way actually sincere? Yet in our most important relationships, we do need to learn how to talk and communicate. An infant's murmurings and gurglings are delightful, to be sure, but we also teach babies how to speak and are happy when they finally utter recognizable words. (Early on, I made lists of the first words spoken by our children.) A baby's spontaneity may change while acquiring vocabulary, but this does not undermine the authenticity of what the baby communicates. Rather, the child's communication deepens so that exchanges are no longer confined to matters of food, warmth, discomfort, and the bathroom, as important as all those are.

Although some of the best things I may say to our children, my spouse, or friends are spontaneous, I also have to learn how to communicate with them. I am still learning how to speak with my wife, even though we have been married for over three decades. Such formation with those we love never comes to an end.

And learned communication is not artificial, even if it is not always spontaneous and extemporaneous. Just because I acquire wisdom about expressing affection or what words to use amid conflict does not mean that those communications are not sincere, true, or authentic. Rather, this helps me to communicate better. In the same way, we all need to grow in how we speak to and with God. Learned language is important. Through the centuries many of the spiritual classics were written by people formed by and immersed in disciplines of common prayer. We cannot separate the wisdom of Benedict or Julian, Athanasius or Evelyn Underhill, Henri Nouwen or Mother Teresa from how they were steeped in and formed by the regular, fixed and formal, rote and repetitive daily prayers of their own common Christian traditions.

The Office is a school of prayer. As we have seen, it teaches us actual words, phrases, and prayers with which to pray. Earlier we reflected on holy habits and on how learned prayers become an automatic part of people's spiritual repertoire. This also argues for memorizing regular prayers so the words can emerge when we need them.

These holy habits school us. When the disciples wanted to learn how to pray and asked Jesus for help, he taught them the Lord's Prayer, a formulaic prayer that was the church's first Office.

The importance of rote and even memorized prayers can be seen in a surprising way in the little book of Jonah. When he was cast into the sea and swallowed by a whale, he prayed, but not spontaneously and extemporaneously. Instead, he uttered psalms, texts that he probably learned in the daily prayers of his faith community. In a moment of crisis and perilous need, he relied on the prayers and prayer forms of his faith tradition. Eugene Peterson comments: "This is amazing. Prayer, which we often suppose is truest when most spontaneous—the raw expression of our human condition without contrivance or artifice—shows up in Jonah when he is in the rawest condition imaginable as learned."[6]

Thus it should not surprise us that even Jesus on the cross, in one of his most heartrending moments, quotes a psalm when he cries out, "My God, my God, why have you forsaken me?" (Mark 15:34b; cf. Psalm 22:1). Learned prayers, then, are important, even vital. This idea is different from

> the prevailing climate of prayer. Our culture presents us with forms of prayer that are mostly self-expression—pouring ourselves out before God or lifting our gratitude to God as we feel the need and have the occasion. Such prayer is dominated by a sense of self. But prayer, mature

prayer, is dominated by a sense of God. Prayer rescues us from a preoccupation with ourselves and pulls us into adoration of and pilgrimage to God.[7]

Learned and memorized texts do more than give words to say and pray. They also teach us prayer's deep rhythms and meanings. Some of the assigned words may be beyond our comfort level: confessing sins or praying for our enemies, for example. And they also lead us to forms of prayer that might not occur to us: praise and thankfulness. They remind us of God's priorities. In so doing, they teach and form us.

Immersion in Scripture
Seeing the Office as a school of prayer, we remember that another key gift is the fact that the texts and words of such practices immerse us in Scripture. It is not just that prayer books encourage us to read, ponder, and meditate on the Bible every day: Psalms, Old Testament readings, biblical canticles, the Gospels. More than that, many of the prayers and responses are derived directly from the Bible. Most of the *Book of Common Prayer* consists of explicit biblical citations or allusions. The same is true for *Take Our Moments and Our Days*. In fact, one reason why it is relatively easy for this prayer book to be translated into other languages is because people elsewhere can just use their own Bible translations to do so.

Along the way in church history, the Bible was treated more and more individualistically, something to read in private devotions. Although personal reading is obviously good, that is too limited for the Bible's purpose and original intention. It is a worship book, written primarily for corporate use. In it are prayers and hymns, stories for challenge and inspiration, confessions of faith, letters of consolation and edification—all meant to be shared in common worship. The Bible was never written with individuals alone in mind; the audience for it was always groups of believers, communities, gathered churches.

Immersion in Scripture familiarizes us with many important Bible texts and themes. Bible readings and prayers may pique curiosity and encourage further study. Such prayer steeps us in Scripture, and we are formed by biblical faith. The editors of *Take Our Moments and Our Days* have always hoped that this prayer book approach would whet people's appetite and lead them into deeper, more extensive Bible reading. In so doing, we join with a wider tradition.

> St. Paul said: "Let the word of Christ, in all its richness, find a home with you" (Colossians 3:16). As we pray the Office day after day, meditating on the word of God, the thought forms and truths of that word take hold of us. Our minds are transformed so that we can discern what is the will of God, "what is good, and acceptable, and perfect"

(Rom[ans] 12:2 [KJV]). The Scriptures begin to soak into our minds and hearts and become part of us. The way we are living is constantly brought into the light of God's Word, to be guided and transformed. In particular, the Scriptures expounding the mystery of the birth, death, and resurrection of our Lord Jesus and of the gift of his Spirit come to determine our thinking and our way of life.[8]

Timely Gifts of the Office

Our culture certainly has many obstacles to prayerfulness. One is the overwhelming "busyness" that so many of us feel and worry about. In the last church that I pastored, congregants often complained of being too busy and asked the church elders to address this issue as a number one priority. Ironically, though the elders agreed to respond, they did not do so for another two years because they themselves could not find the time. Increased busyness is not just imagined. Plenty of evidence suggests that people are working more and more. Even so-called labor-saving devices increase the demands in our lives.

As many of us are divorced from rural rhythms, and as technology helps us overcome darkness, we no longer limit activities to daylight. While this expands opportunities for things to do, it also leads to confusion. We can now shop, work, get entertained, or be reached around the clock, all week long—or 24/7, as some like to say.

Office disciplines, however, offer the opportunity of moving into deeper ways of understanding and—perhaps more important—experiencing time. A life of prayer means dedicating ourselves to a fundamental priority. Otherwise our busy culture will decide for us. Common prayer helps our commitment in a number of ways.

The problem of dealing with time is so large that we cannot overcome it individually. We need companions to accompany us in trying to live differently. In common prayer we enter and end each day in God's rhythms and never do so alone. As other Christians accompany us, we also are encouraged to live faithfully within time.

Many people experience time as random, episodic, accidental, or meaningless. But Christians are encouraged to be deliberate in their approach. We mark our lives by the Christian calendar. On a daily basis, we are immersed in morning and evening rhythms. Fixed-hour prayer enriches our experience of time by purposefully shaping and structuring it according to God's priorities and perspectives.

In the face of overwhelming demands, options, pressures, and opportunities, it often becomes difficult for us to know what to do when. All of us need routines where we do not have to (or do not want to) decide what to do next. By committing ourselves to morning and evening prayer, we choose a key practice at those priority times of the day. The way I originally prayed as a child meant that my devotions depended entirely on my ability, schedule, and motivation. In addition, I had many choices to make in the midst of all that: when to pray, what to pray about, which Scriptures to read. The Office frees us from the stress of so many decisions, decisions, decisions.

Fixed-hour prayer is ideal for busy people. Various versions can easily be prayed in ten to twenty minutes each morning and evening. No matter how much we have to do, almost everyone can afford that much time. *Take Our Moments and Our Days* encourages people to shape the length of their prayers according to their particular circumstances. Lowell Brown wrote to the editors of the Anabaptist prayer books with this testimony: "As a busy person from a town of busy people (New York City), I think *Take Our Moments and Our Days* is the best thing since unprogrammed Quaker meetings."

A little discipline, practiced faithfully, can in the long run make a vast difference in changing one's life. Esther Quinlan is an American Muslim convert who testifies to the joys of observing Muslim fixed-hour prayer (*salat* in Arabic). She writes honestly of how hard it was to acquire this discipline. Learning and growth were gradual but ultimately fruitful. "If we set sail from New York, a tack of only five degrees can make the difference between landing in England or Africa. So it is with the *salat*: the smallest effort acts as a tack, and gradually over a long period of time, the effort brings one to the intended destination."[9]

Common prayer changes our experience of time so that gradually we no longer feel harried, controlled, and pressured, but can live in the rhythms of God's grace.

Ecumenical Gifts

An important benefit of the Office is its ecumenical nature. Not only does it join us in the prayers of Christians through the centuries (the communion of saints), but also with Christians of many traditions around the world. Though it is difficult to achieve Christian unity, institutionally or doctrinally, we can now already be joined in prayers, an anticipation of our worship together in heaven.

Morning and evening prayer's reliance on Scriptures is part of this. For all our differences, Christians agree on the central importance of the Bible. Therefore Christians of many different stripes and traditions can share biblical prayer.

In visits to ecumenical communities with wide international influence—Iona, Taizé, Northumbria— I saw that their daily morning and evening prayer involves Christians from all confessions around the world. Members and guests alike have often commented on the significance of this.

A lifelong Baptist at Northumbria told me of her original discomfort with the liturgical worship of that community. But now she especially appreciates that daily fixed-hour prayer gave her a connection with other Christians and the richness of their traditions.

Such prayer is also the only Roman Catholic liturgy in which all Christians may fully participate. In May 2000, Roman Catholic and Anglican bishops (from thirteen areas of the world) had a historic week-long conference in Mississauga, Ontario, on possible reunification. Although much divided them, they commented on the delight of their "sense of sameness discovered through actions like the daily ritual of morning and evening prayer." Cardinal Edward Idris Cassidy, president of the Vatican's Pontifical Council for Promoting Christian Unity, commented: "We have been together . . . in morning and evening prayer. . . . We are fully in communion in prayer."[10]

The Overseas Ministries Study Center (OMSC, at New Haven, Conn.) has been supporting cross-cultural missions for over eighty years and attracts missionaries and scholars from around the world and across the denominational spectrum. When Eleanor Kreider, one of the editors of *Take Our Moments and Our Days*, spent time there, OMSC was delighted to employ that prayer book regularly in its chapel services and even ordered a number of copies for on-going use. This prayer book had an unprecedented appeal for visitors. Baptists and Pentecostals who were more familiar with spontaneous prayer appreciated the services' explicit reliance on Scripture and room for extemporaneity. But more liturgical folks—Catholics, Orthodox, Anglicans, and Lutherans—recognized and appreciated the morning and evening rhythms of prayer. Years later, the Center still uses it occasionally as part of a rich mix of traditions, according to Jonathan Bonk, executive director of OMSC.

The Gifts of Solidarity and Support

Christians have the option of expressing solidarity by praying similar words and themes with other believers. When I traveled in the British Isles, I was struck by the dispersed-communities models of Iona, Northumbria, and Aidan and Hilda. Each group is made up of people who live at some distance from one another but have made mutual pledges about their lifestyles, priorities, and ways to be accountable to each other for their promises. A primary commitment in all the dispersed communities is shared daily prayer. People are sustained in their faithfulness by being prayerfully connected with each other.

Christian prayer is actually intended to be corporate, not primarily private and individualistic. The only prayer that Jesus gave us begins with "our"; we find the collective dimension in "we" and "us," but not in "mine," "I," or "me." Common prayer means intentionally joining with others.

For years I tried hard to be a person of prayer but found it difficult to keep my discipline alone. Yet when I vowed before monks at St. Gregory's Abbey to be committed to daily prayer, I made great strides in this demanding discipline. I was better able to pray regularly, not just because I took a vow promising to do so, but also because I knew that brother monks at St. Gregory's Abbey were praying with me and for me.

An example from another sphere of my life illustrates this. Some years ago I joined a writers' group for the first time. We met weekly, and I found that their perspectives improved my efforts. They kept me accountable about my writing, since it was regularly my turn to share work with them. Thus I had to produce. But there was another payoff too. Writing, like prayer, can be devastatingly solitary. One sits in front of a blank computer screen or an empty page and wonders, "Why do I bother?" Sometimes prayer feels the same way: lonely, empty, and pointless. But now I knew that in the town where I lived, others in my writers' group were struggling with the very same issues. Such awareness encouraged me to keep going. Not coincidentally, I completed my first book within a year of joining that group. In the spiritual life, as in writing, it is a gift to draw upon and practice disciplines in solidarity and community with fellow believers.

Phyllis Tickle has written of this with her usual elegant eloquence:

> The prayers I was offering were the same ones being offered by thousands of Christians in my time zone at exactly the same time I was offering them, as if we were indeed a cloud of witnesses and a great company of believers; amazing that the prayers I was offering were in large part the same prayers of praise and worship that my Lord had

prayed and offered; amazing that increasingly as I prayed I could hear, as one friend of mine now says, "a thousand's thousand voices" joining mine across all that is or has been or will be.[11]

Someone once said that those who pray with the support of others are like mountain climbers roped together. Those who pray alone resemble individual pioneers who learn by trial and error, without the help and guidance of those who have gone ahead. With a common discipline or Office, we move beyond privatized, solitary, personal devotions to praying with other believers, not only around the world but also with the entire communion of saints. The Office reminds us that no matter what our race, country, location, denomination, or liturgical preference might happen to be, as Christians we have more in common than not.

A former parishioner learned the value of mutual connection, commitment, and support in an unexpected way. She joined our Easter season project where a small group committed themselves to daily morning and evening prayer. At that time, her husband was traveling two or more weeks a month overseas. They each bought the prayer book, both telling me more than once that it was not actually their "style." During regular separations, though, this shared discipline was a strong connection for them as they emailed back and forth commentaries and reflections on the readings and prayers of the day.

Solidarity in common prayer operates in several ways. It gives support and encouragement in prayers. A friend visited a monastery a long time ago. He told me afterward that the oft-repeated doxology "Glory to the Father, and to the Son, and to the Holy Spirit, as it was in the beginning, is now, and will be forever" gave him deep comfort. Whenever he remembered the monks praying that, he would recite that short sentence too and take heart.

Common prayer even brings unity where we might not want it. At times I was involved in prayers where someone was present whom I disliked or with whom I was in conflict. I would not have chosen to have that person there; I did not invite them, and I was not always pleased to see them, truth be told. But God's wisdom works differently from ours. I found that I could even pray with and beside people with whom I disagree. (It would probably be harder for both parties if that person or I made up our own prayers, but following an "objective," imposed program was helpful.) Morning and evening prayer is especially challenging here when we pray, "Forgive us our sins, as we forgive those who sin against us." Intriguingly, as we have already noted, this was one reason that Benedict wanted the Lord's Prayer prayed every morning and evening: so the monks would remember the importance of mutual forgiveness.

Finally, prayer is hard to do without the upholding of others. Brother Émile of Taizé told me:

People are not going to be able to persevere in personal prayer. In regular common prayer, you join together and take your part—every week, month, or day. Discouragement is too easy today. But in common prayer you support one another. We are never all at the same place during any time. This week I support you, and next week I need your support.

Two-Way Blessings

We praise and worship God because God is worthy. "Worship" literally means "ascribing worth." God calls us to such worship, and probably nothing further needs to be said. This in itself is argument enough for daily morning and evening prayer. But the truth is that our praise and worship of God also brings many blessings our way, as we saw in this chapter when we looked at the gifts of common prayer.

When I did a pulpit exchange in the Netherlands years ago, a congregant there asked me about the English word "blessing." In Dutch, the comparable word is *zegen*. But there only people can be blessed. Blessing is divine, conferred by God. This parishioner was confused about how "blessing" is used in English, especially when we speak of "blessing God." The English understanding of the word is broader and includes a sense of thanking, praising, glorifying, and adoring—all primary elements of the liturgy of the hours.

I am fond of Dutch, my mother tongue. I am even happy and comforted by the sound of it when I travel through an airport and hear KLM Royal Dutch Airlines make a simple boarding announcement in that language. But in this matter of blessing, here I prefer English. Because the truth is that blessings are seldom one-directional. If I live and minister in a way that blesses or brings blessing to others at home, in the seminary, at church, in my neighborhood, then I know that I am often blessed in the process. People who serve others often say that they feel blessed in what they do.

Prayer and worship also work in this two-way fashion. In blessing God with our prayers and offerings (a word, remember, that is closely related to "Office"), we ourselves experience blessings. The process goes on and on, since as we bless God because of the blessings we receive, then we have all the more reason to praise and be thankful.

The Office can certainly be hard to pray. It has its challenges, to be sure. Yet I find it hard not to be enthusiastic about what is offered. In God's paradoxical and upside-down economy, the cost is often its own reward, as we can see from an experiment conducted in a small rural Mennonite congregation.

Testing the Waters

Experiments in Praying Morning and Evening Prayer

Sheila's life fell apart. She was a lifelong Christian with dreams of having a loving family, secure work, and a reliable income. Yet in midlife, during a few devastating months, she lost almost everything. Separated from her spouse, not by her own choice or preference, she moved away from her children and the family home into an ugly, cheaply furnished apartment, all alone. Time passed slowly for her there. Furthermore, she had trouble holding down regular work and so also experienced economic insecurity.

Without job or family, weighed down by grief and regret, Sheila had little in the way of structure, rhythm, or purpose. During these days she learned for the first time about traditional Christian disciplines of common prayer. Prayer and Bible reading had always been important for her, at least in theory. Yet she was never able to maintain a regular practice.

While struggling with her midlife troubles, she began to pray every morning and evening. Scriptures came alive as she read and engaged them in the midst of her own challenging circumstances. She had a lot to talk over with God.

Then she realized something else. She heard church bells ring at regular intervals. They had always rung, but she had never paid attention to them before. Now that she knew about the daily office, she recognized them as a call to prayer. And she took heart, even though she was not even completely sure which church was the source of the ringing.

In a trying situation, Sheila was ministered to by an often-overlooked and sadly ignored Christian tradition: fixed-hour prayer. She practiced it privately and yet was encouraged in it by the wider church.

If We Try It, Will They Like It?

I love ideas and dreaming. In elementary school, I sometimes got into trouble because I had difficulty paying attention to what happened in class or was said by the teacher. I spent a lot of time looking out the window and getting lost in my fantasies. I have learned along the way that it is important to test and apply my theories and theology.

As a pastor, I wanted to know whether my emerging convictions about morning and evening prayer could be implemented more broadly than just in my own devotional life. Was it possible to uncover this practice for a group of Mennonites, even though they were not familiar with it?

So one year, in my former congregation during the season of Easter until Pentecost, a dozen people committed themselves to praying common morning and evening prayer five times a week, using a Carmelite prayer book, *Companion to the Breviary*. People filled out questionnaires and kept spiritual journals to help me understand what this experience was like for them. As well, we gathered on Wednesdays to pray evening prayers together and to recapture a lost tradition of midweek prayer meetings. We shared about how the project was going, and I taught the group about the Office's history and theology, developing prayer disciplines, and the challenges of being prayerful amid our busy lives.

This was a rewarding enterprise for pastor and congregant alike. People learned a lot and acquired a new way to pray, and many commented on how this experience challenged them to be more disciplined in their spiritual lives. Some said they had never before considered spending this much time praying, but they found that twenty to thirty minutes was quite doable once or even twice a day. Here too, you may remember, was the congregant who was able to pray for the first time since a family tragedy over two years earlier.

Some certainly did struggle with an "imposed prayer" of so many words. But others who could never previously maintain daily devotions were now able to do so. Several were pleasantly surprised by this ability. One learned so much from this way of praying that she used its praise-listening-response outline to structure spontaneous prayers when she went outside for long walks. Most reported growing comfortable with the daily office. A few saw that this practice works well even, and perhaps especially so, in a busy lifestyle. One was surprised at how easy it all was.

By the end of our time together, most said that they would not continue common prayer twice a day but would nevertheless spend more time praying in the future. Over a year later I checked and found that four people were still regularly using the prayer book. Everyone in the group told me how this experience motivated them to be more deliberate in their prayer life and met their longing and hope for spiritual growth.

Toward the end of our time, we had several offers from people outside the group to buy any prayer books that project participants no longer wanted. But no one was willing to sell their copies! Several planned to use their prayers either in the morning or evening, and one intended to use the book in her upcoming retirement. A few began thinking about shaping a version of common prayer that took into consideration Mennonite church history, traditions, and hymns.

People were struck by how commitment to others and praying with them helped them maintain a discipline. One said: "If I hadn't promised to do this, I wouldn't make it." They wondered how the church could keep encouraging and supporting people to pray together.

Another benefit of our practice was that participants reflected much on Psalms because morning and evening prayer relies so heavily on them. One person began the project by saying she hated the Psalms, but she and others studied a Walter Brueggemann book for perspective. As a result, several actually wanted more psalms in Sunday worship and dreamed about learning to sing or chant them. They came to a new appreciation of our most ancient prayer book. Another wrote in her journal, "Praying Psalms which often recite salvation history gives me a sense of being part of a long history of struggle and mercy. My struggles are a small bit of this broad story, which leads to hope and trust in God's guidance and mercy." One called this a good "practice to ground myself in Christian identity."

Many noticed that this way of praying affected their daily life. A participant said, "I feel more grateful for each day and am more aware of God's goodness as I read the Psalms and prayers." Another observed that it "made me more aware of God's constant presence." Others spoke of having a greater sense of purpose and direction as they went about their various responsibilities. One was helped to pray for a wider range of concerns than usual. Still another wrote in her journal, "In daily prayer there is recurring longing to live truthfully, justly, according to God's call in my life." Someone else said: "Frequently words from Scripture stayed with me throughout the day."

One spoke of how this worked in a busy life: "The daily prayer was helpful because it reminded me to stop and read and pray." Another said, "Sometimes it was just going through the motions, especially at night when I was tired. I still think it was okay: a sleepy good-night to God, but a turning of intention nonetheless." This person was strongly helped by the prayers: "Some days I felt so calm and centered, like I was balanced on the edge of something (a tightrope, a pin), and the feeling of balance stayed a long time."

Some felt freed. They no longer had to figure everything out: what, when, or for how long to pray. One said: "It was all there: I didn't need to look any further." Another observed, "I could just read it over and get as much out of it as possible." A third summarized matters this way:

> The Office covers it all efficiently. I don't have to be worried that I've missed something. It's measurable. I know when I'm done and thus have freedom from guilt.

Many said this helped and freed them to pray more.

There were implications for worship. Several now felt better prepared for Sundays. One reported that daily prayers made "Sunday worship seem less out of sync with the rest of life." Another observed that morning and evening prayer is not as "I-centered" as some contemporary worship. Several said that the Easter season (not normally stressed by Mennonites) now had deeper meaning.

This experience also created appropriate dissatisfaction. Some were now less happy with how they had prayed previously. One had never thought before of praying every evening, for example, even though that now seemed to her to be an obvious option.

I do not pretend that people loved everything. This was obviously not the case since most did not commit themselves to twice-daily prayer over the long-term future. A perplexing reality was that often the thing one person most liked (e.g., Psalms or repetition) was also the very aspect someone else liked the least. This reminds us that such prayer does not work the same for all. Furthermore, it suggests that common prayer, like Sunday worship, is richest if it is sufficiently varied to help people engage and connect in different ways.

By the end of our time, several said that they would miss having others praying together at similar times, with the same content, and interceding for each other.

While many in that group began with some suspicion of this unfamiliar manner of praying, by the end most rated this experience of prayer as "good." A number of them commented on how much they liked and felt comfortable with the Office.

This small experiment confirmed the importance of churches finding and generating ways to meet people's need to pray, to call and remind people to pray regularly, and to build a sense of praying along with others.

Such prayer can be hard—as shown in struggles discussed in sharing times and in journals. Yet some who could never previously maintain prayer learned a new way now and were surprised to see that they were able to keep this priority. For the first time several saw that commitment and discipline are possible. A few commented that the Office is achievable, for some even easy. One wrote in the last questionnaire:

> It suddenly seems to me there's really no excuse. It . . . felt calm and relaxed. I think I'll keep on going [after this project]. I like this book [the Breviary].

(Years later this participant was still praying the Office—and this from a person who previously found it difficult to maintain a daily discipline.)

People gave serious (and often new) thought about how to pray. Even those who did not continue using the Breviary resolved to spend more time praying than they had before our experiment together. This common practice encouraged a longing for spiritual growth; it motivated people to work on and improve their time with God.

Thus I urge churches to find more means to meet people's need to pray, and to call and remind people to do so every day. The forms we tested were not suitable for everyone in the study group, so I do not suggest that it should be imposed as an obligation on all Christians. Even eloquent advocates of twice-daily prayer admit that it is challenging and not for everyone. Yet it is deeply rooted in the New Testament church and needs and deserves more attention.

This lost treasure of daily morning and evening prayer had much to offer a small group that had known virtually nothing about it before. They were pleasantly surprised by discoveries, their faith was enriched, and their prayer was enhanced. Many could benefit by uncovering this ancient rhythm of prayer, an important heritage of all Christians.

Recovering Daily Prayer

Sheila discovered the deeper meaning of the familiar sound of church bells as a reminder of God's presence, call, and invitation to pray. We have seen that there is an old Anglican tradition that bells are rung when the Office begins. Not only are the bells a call to prayer; they can also be a loving gesture to tell one's neighbors that they are in our prayers.

There are many ways to invite people into our spiritual life. For one special occasion, David Adam of Lindisfarne wrote a prayer about his island community and distributed it throughout the town. Neighbors posted it in their homes and prayed it whenever they heard the church's bell. They found it significant even as a discipline for just a few weeks. Others continued to observe it for a long time.

In an era of pilgrimage and seeking, when many look to ancient Christian resources—or elsewhere when we do not provide them—and struggle with deep questions, the church needs to provide havens of prayer and help people by creating structures and support for their spiritual life.

John Westerhoff III and William Willimon discuss the challenge of recovering daily prayer:

> If the Church does nothing else for the world other than to keep open a house, symbolic of the homeland of the soul, where in-season and out-of-season people can gather daily to pray, it is doing the social order the greatest possible service. So long as the Church bids people to daily meditation and prayer, and provides a simple and credible vehicle for the devotional life, it need not question its place, mission, and influence in the world. If it loses faith in the daily offering of common prayer, it need not look to its avocations to save it, for it is dead at heart.
>
> Nothing may be more important than a rebirth of daily morning and evening common prayer in every church.[1]

Once I would have considered their conclusion to be exaggerated, but my own practice, work with congregants, travel to Christian communities on both sides of the Atlantic, ministry with seminary students and colleagues, and theological reflections all now convince me that they are right.

By uncovering this lost treasure, the church takes one more step toward the vision of the psalmist (in 113:3, *The Grail Psalms*)[2] who proclaims,

> From the rising of the sun to its setting
> praised be the name of the Lord.

Epilogue
Take Our Moments and Our Days
The Creation of a Contemporary Anabaptist Prayer Book

*e*ven though I slowly grew more and more convinced about the theological and pastoral importance of reclaiming common morning and evening prayer, I needed a lot of nudging from others along the way. "A little help from my friends" was not nearly enough for me. I had no idea that the last sentences of chapter 9, my final words in *The Rhythm of God's Grace*, might actually spark responses within a few years. And I was in no way able to do this alone.

To tell this story I need to begin some time ago. On Labor Day 1999, Lorna and I took our adolescents out for supper at our favorite restaurant in Kitchener to mark the end of summer. Erin and Paul were returning to school the next day. I mentioned that a grant application had been on my desk for months but I had decided not to pursue it. There was only a week left before the deadline. It was a busy time of year. And really, did I need to think up other projects in my already-full life? I figured that Lorna would be relieved. Normally she is appropriately cautious about my commitments since I often take on more than is sensible. This time, however, she was unexpectedly adamant with another view-point: "I think you need to do this." This was the first unexpected nudge, a suppertime conversation that eventually changed my life.

So over the next seven days I carefully but hurriedly drafted a grant application and recruited necessary references. Two months later I learned that the Louisville Institute was funding me to research daily morning and evening prayer by sponsoring travels to Lindisfarne, Iona, Taizé, Northumbria, Christ in the Desert, and St. John's Abbey in Collegeville, Minnesota. That was the second nudge.

Since I was then a pastor, the Mennonite press publicized this small windfall. I was caught off guard when various church leaders from around North America—pastors, professors, denominational officials, writers, editors—contacted me in response to news of the grant. They all wrote of the importance of daily morning and evening prayer in their own spiritual lives. Many told me which prayer book they used and why. And they began asking whether there might someday be an Anabaptist rendition. This was my first hint that others might already have a substantial interest in such work. I was hardly the only Anabaptist who experienced the benefits of common prayer and saw the unexpected potential of such prayer practices. That was the third unexpected nudge.

Around that time I met Nelson Kraybill, then president of Associated Mennonite Biblical Seminary

(AMBS) at Elkhart, Indiana. We were at a birthday party and had a long conversation about daily morning and evening prayer, of all things. Perhaps that makes us geeks, but neither of us would worry about that. He'd heard the news of the Louisville funding and asked me about recommended resources and prayer books.

Two years later I was teaching pastoral theology at AMBS. Several students urged me to facilitate common prayer at the school. I hesitated. I was in a new job in an unfamiliar setting, working up courses that I had never taught before. I checked with Lorna about this possibility, and once more she said, "I think you need to do this." And so I was nudged a fourth time.

I began meeting with students, staff, and faculty early on Wednesday mornings. We prayed with the *People's Companion to the Breviary* and sang hymns in four-part harmony. A group of us visited the Indianapolis Carmelites who had created that prayer book. Here again I saw how this form of common prayer was deeply significant for a number of people.

In the meantime, I finished writing *The Rhythm of God's Grace*, which was published in the spring of 2003. Nelson Kraybill began talking with me more about the need for Anabaptists to consider creating a prayer book. I had once toyed with the idea of developing one myself. After *Rhythm* was published, some friends persistently proposed this idea to me. But I do not have poetic facility with language: I am no David Adam. And I was daunted by the size of the task. Besides, my theology insists that the best prayer books written for communities of faith also grow out of communities of faith. I decided not to try such a thing by myself. But Nelson's nudge was compelling, even more so when he found modest funding to sponsor such an event.

So he and I invited a group of Canadian and American Mennonite leaders. Around twenty people came together in September 2003: pastors, poets, editors, theologians, Bible scholars, historians, writers, musicians, liturgists. We met in Nelson's home for a weekend. He is a genius at process, and we put together a careful discernment schedule. We tackled one main question: Is it time for Mennonites to develop a prayer book? But first we had other processing in mind. So we spent time in learning together from Arnold Snyder about sixteenth-century Anabaptist prayer practices and their concordances that aided Bible memorization. We discussed *The Rhythm of God's Grace* and how that work was being received. Eleanor Kreider and Marlene Kropf spoke of their dream in the early 1990s to develop a prayer book, but their sad conclusion back then was that the time was not yet right.

Nelson and I wanted to carefully give adequate time to having all the pieces in place before trying to move to clarity and discernment. We soon discovered, however, that individuals had made up their minds before they had come. During breaks, people nudged: "Come on, let's get on with this." They felt no need to test a consensus. It was already clear to the gathered consultants: Yes, it is time to do this. That was the most dramatic and telling nudge of all.

The weekend moved quickly from there to issues and practical details. We talked about which Bible translation should be used, again expecting controversy, but the group unanimously preferred the *New Revised Standard Version*. We pondered whether Mennonites needed to develop a Bible lectionary but decided that was not something for us to tackle.

We considered what would be worthy priorities for an Anabaptist prayer book and developed the following:

- Amply using Scripture, especially in ways that would encourage pray-ers to learn texts by heart. Prayer should be Scripture-saturated.
- Focusing on the life, words, and teachings of Jesus, given their centrality to Anabaptist convictions.
- Encouraging prayers to be accompanied by singing.
- Loving attention to language.
- Being inclusive in terminology and texts.
- Developing a book that was also lovely to look at and hold, since this reminds us that what we are doing is worthwhile.
- Widely testing whatever we try throughout the church.

We also agreed on a number of practical considerations:

- The book should be affordable. We would seek patrons to subsidize publication if necessary.
- The volume should be a good size for portability. Large, unwieldy books are hard to carry or hold and are even worse for traveling.
- It is best to have all-in-one services. Too many prayer books require multiple ribbons or bookmarks.
- There needs to be good binding that will stand up to repeated use. The spine should fall open easily so that the book can lie flat without breaking.

Finally, the ad hoc group appointed a committee (Arthur Boers, Gloria Jost, Eleanor Kreider, and John Rempel) to draft a prayer book for wide testing throughout the North American church. And so I was nudged once more.

How and Where to Begin?

The prayer book committee quickly moved into action. We considered the consultation's findings and dreamed about how to implement the various recommendations. We wanted to offer services that take perhaps fifteen minutes to pray, while giving people the option to shorten or lengthen the time as appropriate.

We had a head start, really, because Eleanor

Kreider had been pondering these kinds of possibilities for years and had many ideas and suggestions for us. At home, her kitchen table became buried by sheets full of plans and possibilities. It is hard to overemphasize the central role of Eleanor in all this—practically, theologically, and theoretically. She is the mother of this project, and I doubt it would have happened without her.

Our committee decided that the prayer services should have a fourfold pattern: call to praise, call to Jesus, call to discipleship, and finally a call to prayer of thanks and intercession. We lit upon the idea of developing a two-week cycle for ordinary time. In keeping with our hope to emphasize the words and teachings of Jesus, so central for Mennonites, we decided that one week would revolve around the Lord's Prayer and the other around the Beatitudes (the latter of special priority for Anabaptists). We would provide short Scripture passages for pondering, space for reflecting on the biblical words, and suggested hymns.

We also planned to emphasize particular theological themes for each day of the week, a common approach in many prayer books. This is a way of cycling through salvation history on a weekly basis. We decided on the following format:

- Sunday: Easter, resurrection, *Christus Victor*
- Monday: Pentecost, new creation, the era of the Holy Spirit

- Tuesday: Incarnation, God with us (in brother/sister, neighbor, enemy)
- Wednesday: Epiphany, God revealed in Jesus Christ, passion for peace and justice
- Thursday: Lent, the Christian walk, journeying with Christ
- Friday: Holy Week, passion and mission of Christ, cost of following Jesus
- Saturday: Reign of God, communion of saints, every tribe and nation

We set to work, drafting and developing services. Within a year, we had a small (118 pages), plain white, generic-looking, self-published volume containing a two-week cycle that was printed by Pandora Press. Its simple austerity was offset by Barbara and James Nelson Gingerich's careful layout and design and an attractive calligraphy font developed just for us by Lois Siemens for various headings. The layout was used in the following versions as well. When Herald Press joined the project, Gwen Stamm did the calligraphy on the book covers and on the divider pages.

From the beginning, James was a key behind-the-scenes collaborator. He formatted the services in all the prayer book drafts, up to and including the final form of the text in both finished volumes. Whenever any of us wanted to experiment with a service in a particular setting, he always eagerly and cheerfully formatted a booklet version.

Our first small prayer book was widely distributed. We used it for morning prayers at AMBS, and committee members brought it to their local churches and small groups. Members of the original consultation employed it in various settings too. We recruited other people who might be interested in testing our work. At the back of the book we included a questionnaire asking about people's patterns of praying with the services, what was appreciated, what was difficult, what it was like to pray with others, how this affected one's devotional life, whether this was particularly suited to certain age groups or traditions, and about suggestions for improvement. Services were posted at websites—AMBS, Mennonite Church Canada, and Mennonite Church USA—so that there was wide accessibility.

We eagerly studied and compiled the many responses that came from throughout North America and also from farther away: France, Lithuania, Guatemala, India, and Finland. We heard not only from Mennonites and other Anabaptists but also from various evangelicals and even liturgically astute Benedictines. People began inquiring about translating these services into other languages, including Lithuanian and French, and we happily agreed. Later the editors were approached for permission to translate the prayers into Japanese, German, and Spanish as well. (Since the services are largely based in and derived from Scripture texts, conversion into other languages is relatively straightforward: simply employ the Bible translation of one's own language.)

Then we began working on a four-week cycle of prayers and services for ordinary time, adding two weeks, basing one week on the parables of Jesus and the other reflecting on his signs and wonders. We compiled the results in loose-leaf binders. Gloria Jost decided to step down from our committee; she lived in Washington (all the other editors were in Elkhart) and in the meantime had decided to become an Episcopalian. We also received generous funding from the Anabaptist Foundation of Canada.

In April 2005 we held another consultation. Again about twenty people gathered, this time in my home. The group was grateful for how quickly we had produced a draft prayer book and affirmed the process of soliciting widespread feedback and responses. They also named a number of issues. For various reasons, they were not satisfied with our four-week draft. Good concerns were raised: Was enough attention given to the Psalms? Were Scripture choices superficial? Were we appropriately careful about inclusive language? Was there enough room for extemporaneity? Were services sufficiently missional and evangelical?

In other words, this was a strong start, but there was much more work to do. The committee invited additional members. Barbara Nelson Gingerich came on board with her impressive combination of theological acuity, publishing experience, love of worship and language, and an impressive work ethic. From the beginning Barbara and her husband, James, as mentioned above, had already been much in the background as they helped with the layout of various early drafts. We also recognized that our work was deficient because none of the committee members were Scripture scholars. AMBS New Testament professor Mary Schertz agreed to join us as well; she often consulted other Bible scholars, especially Perry Yoder and Ben Ollenburger. When Mary later went on a yearlong sabbatical, AMBS New Testament professor emeritus Willard Swartley filled in; he was one of our original consultants.

Prayer Book, Take Two
We had probably been a little too complacent about the speed and ease with which we drafted our two-week prayer book. Expanding this to four weeks was more complicated than we first imagined. And the second ad hoc consultation actually *rejected* our four-week draft and sent us back to the drawing board. Nevertheless, the reconfigured group of five editors engaged the challenges.

We reworked our prayer-service model and revisited our four-week draft. Mary Schertz helped us reconsider prior Scripture selections, looking for deeper theological affinities and congruence. For the opening psalms in the services, we decided to use the translation of *The Grail Psalms*.[1] Old Testament scholars told us that this was an especially reliable translation, capturing both the original sense and meaning of the psalms and also their poetic rhythms and feel. And we appreciated the attention to inclusivity.

We lengthened the Scripture passages and simplified the service structure to a threefold call (call to praise, call to discipleship, and call to prayer). We made room early in each service for extemporaneous thanksgivings and shortened the intercessions.

Our meetings included vigorous discussions about doxologies, hymn choices, Scripture selections, and inclusive language. But we were pleased that our committee brought and blended various realms of expertise and passion: theological and historical perspectives, pastoral priorities, comprehensive scriptural sensitivity, and liturgical sensibility. We knew that too often liturgists and Scripture scholars had competing priorities, but our team brought all these vital perspectives into necessary and fruitful conversation.

Along the way, we continued to put our services on the Web, encouraging people to download, test, and modify them. This was not about intellectual property. Rather, we were trying to offer resources as a gift to the wider church. By December 1995, we published our second draft (a thousand copies), a four-week cycle for Ordinary Time. This sturdier edition included a laminated bookmark with two versions of the Lord's Prayer. Again we appended a questionnaire inviting feedback.

Eventually this version morphed into our first officially published volume, *Take Our Moments and Our Days: An Anabaptist Prayer Book: Ordinary Time* (Herald Press, 2007). With a flexible faux leather cover and two ribbons, it looked and felt more like a traditional prayer book. In contrast with the previous four-week version, this one included more resources, added hymn suggestions (after impressive input by Ken Nafziger and Rebecca Slough), room for praying versions of the doxology, and fine collects penned by Gayle Gerber Koontz, Andrew Kreider, Lois Siemens, and Darrin Snyder Belousek.

But our work was not yet done. People repeatedly asked for services connected to the church seasons. This turned out to be the most massive undertaking of all. We developed prayer cycles for Advent, Christmas, Epiphany, Lent, Holy Week, Easter, and Pentecost. A 649-page, paperback volume was copublished by the Institute for Mennonite Studies and Herald Press in 2007. It eventually sold out, and was revised for publication in 2010, along with a new version of the first volume for Ordinary Time. The prayer books include musical settings for the various calls; we commissioned the music by James E. Clemens.

Recorded versions of four services were also posted on the AMBS website, using the musical settings by Clemens. The services were prepared by using AMBS readers and singers from Assembly Mennonite Church (Goshen).

Other projects, possibilities, questions, and issues remain. Are there ways to adapt the services appropriately for children and youth? Even though the prayers are translated into other languages, does this remain a primarily Eurocentric approach? Does such prayer appeal across different classes and various intellectual interests? These matters need on-going discernment and testing.

My own role as coordinating editor often shifted during the years of editing and consulting. Sometimes other responsibilities took me away for periods of time. Finally, in 2008 I was first waylaid by health concerns and then accepted a teaching position in Canada, both of which made it impractical for me to continue as one of the editors. Eleanor, Barbara, John, and Mary carried on the work.

Observations along the Way

The committee and our consultants noticed a number of things about how *Take Our Moments and Our Days* was received and employed.

We received testimonies from throughout North America and indeed from around the world that testified that our work strengthened the spiritual lives of others. And not only Mennonites responded. We heard from Baptists, Christian Reformed pastors, Benedictine nuns and monks, Disciples of Christ, Pentecostals, Roman Catholics, and Episcopalians, to name only a few. People tested and experimented with these prayers in Sunday school classes, prayer meetings, and small group settings. One church recorded a CD version so that members who commuted could pray along with the recording while they traveled. Some churches met weekly to use the prayers during particular seasons, such as Advent or Lent.

Because the services are already planned, more

people felt empowered to lead worship and devotional times. Lowell Brown wrote us, "With next to no set-up time required, I found it to be an easy, varied, and meaningful way to facilitate a small group gathering." In one family, the teenage boys actually argued about whose turn it was to lead the prayers since both were so eager to do so! The structure gave timid Christians courage to guide the prayer of others.

We noticed that more and more Mennonite meetings and conferences were using our services for worship and devotionals at the beginning of gatherings and regularly during multiday events. We heard appreciation for the quality of these prayers as opening devotionals. We were pleased to see Mennonite World Conference (MWC) taking an interest in this work, publishing articles about it in *Courier*, and using services in various international gatherings.

Appreciation was expressed for how the widening circles of intercession are structured: suggestions for petitions about ourselves and those dear to us, our community and neighbors, the church around the world, and nations and governments. People noted that this helped them pray more broadly and deeply than they tend to do when they rely solely on their own personal prayer lists or whatever arises spontaneously while praying.

The language of the prayers was also affecting Sundays. We were pleasantly surprised when we heard pastors and worship leaders employ parts of our liturgies during weekly gatherings. Intercessions and calls to worship, for example, were often based on suggestions from *Take Our Moments and Our Days*. A number of congregations adapted entire *Take Our Moments and Our Days* services for Sunday worship.

There were other benefits too. People often reported carrying away particular Scripture phrases or verses from the prayers that then informed and inspired them through the day. They literally learned texts by heart. Dave Vroege, a Christian Reformed pastor in Nova Scotia, wrote: "On my walk to my church each morning, I'll take a line from the morning prayers, adapt it to a sung prayer I know, and use it to continue praying as I walk through neighbourhoods and down city streets—powerful stuff!"

Or pray-ers found consolation in various refrains. One correspondent testified that the sentence "You are good to those who wait for you, to all who seek you" became especially important. She had been praying with the prayer book regularly for some time when a terrible tragedy happened in her family. This line, already deeply embedded in her heart, helped her to trust God in the midst of terrifying and perplexing circumstances.

At annual AMBS Pastors' Weeks, we offered *Take Our Moments and Our Days* prayers each and every morning. I paid attention to who showed up and how they prayed. One thing especially struck me. The Mennonite denomination, like many others, sometimes feels divided between those who stress peace and social justice concerns and those who emphasize personal piety and the importance of missions and evangelism. Sadly, these two groups can become silos that do not always communicate well with each other and may not naturally choose to worship and pray together. But a wide theological spectrum was represented at our gatherings. If nothing else, the prayer book brought together people who did not otherwise naturally connect for prayer and worship.

And there is one more gift that I find especially remarkable. Another way to "group" Christians is by dividing them into those who feel comfortable praying aloud and those who do not. Sometimes this is a matter of theological self-selection. But I have seen that this also has to do with personality, life experience, and self-confidence. The carefully structured frame of the prayer book, which provides room and suggestions for oral prayer, actually frees up and equips more people, helping them dare to pray out loud. I often noticed that the safe setting of prayer book worship taught people to claim their own voice in prayer, people who might not otherwise say aloud their thanksgivings and intercessions.

An Emerging Mennonite Prayer-Book Spirituality
When I studied at AMBS in the 1980s, fellow student Rebecca Slough (later my colleague at AMBS when we both taught there) tried to gather students, staff, and faculty for regular prayers with a Taizé prayer book. Like most AMBSers back then, I was not interested.

Marlene Kropf and Eleanor Kreider, deeply respected Mennonite church leaders, first dreamed of a possible prayer book in the early 1990s. Yet they ruefully concluded that the time was not yet right.

A decade later, however, Rebecca, Marlene, and Eleanor—with the help of many others—contributed to and helped develop various versions of *Take Our Moments and Our Days* and ensuing projects too.

Prayer-book spirituality, as we know, is not for everyone. It never was and never will be. Yet the hard work of scores of folks and the nudging of the Spirit have helped Mennonites, Anabaptists, and many others uncover and claim this form of prayer for the renewal of personal and corporate spirituality, small group and congregational life.

The best response I know to such good news comes from the daily Thanksgiving in the prayer book itself:

My heart is ready, O God:
    I will sing your praise.

Appendix A
Tips for Praying Morning and Evening Prayer

For those not accustomed to common prayer practices, the following suggestions provide a place to start.

Finding Your Way, Learning the Structure
If you or the members of your group struggle with how to proceed or find your way in a chosen prayer book, look first to see if there are instructions in the book itself. Many versions have helps or guides near the beginning.

Look also at Appendix B in this book on the "Structure and Content of Morning and Evening Prayer." This will help you understand the intended order. Chances are that when you know the structure and flow of the prayers, they will make more sense and will feel much less confusing.

It might also be useful to know that weekdays often have themes.

Enhancing Your Prayers
You may want to take your tradition's hymnbook and find hymns particularly suited to morning and evening prayers. These too can enrich your time of devotion. *Take Our Moments and Our Days* lists

carefully chosen selections. And you are free—and encouraged!—to make your own choices.

If possible, try to pray your prayers at approximately the same time each day, when you can be relatively free of disturbances or interruptions and can ignore the phone or doorbell. If necessary, note your prayer appointment in your datebook. Almost no one argues with or even questions our calendars. In *Space for God*, Don Postema reports that he used to write "Prayer" in a calendar time slot but found that too easy to overlook: "Now I write '7–7:30 a.m.—God.' Somehow that's a little harder to neglect."[1]

Many also find it helpful to set aside a special place for prayer. Such a spot (it need not be a room; a corner, a cushion, or a chair may do) should be visually conducive to prayer. One can add a flower, candle, rock, icon, or piece of art to enhance the worshipful quality. Try not to be in a place that is cluttered or that reminds you of all the work you have to do. (Appendix C also has suggestions pertaining to making a space prayerful.)

Start Modestly and Proceed Slowly
Many prayer sequences can be prayed in ten to fifteen minutes. Begin shorter and slowly expand as you are able; that is better than starting too ambitiously and becoming discouraged. Be realistic about how much time you can pray, and set modest goals. Take this in small steps.

By the way, C. W. McPherson, in his excellent

book, recommends beginning with either morning or evening prayer for a time, perhaps several weeks or months, before trying to do both regularly.[2] It is too hard to go from not saying common prayer to then saying it twice a day. You may risk being frustrated and discouraged, and you might give up entirely. Start shorter and build as you can.

The length of your prayers will depend on whether you add periods of silence or spend time in free prayer, conversing with God. Some prayer books give ideas about where to include silences. In *Take Our Moments*, such pauses are suggested after thanksgivings, confession (in the evening), Scripture reading, and during several places in the intercession. Pray slowly and deliberately.

If you are by yourself, do not feel compelled to do everything at a steady pace. John Brook recommends, "If a phrase or word catches you, stay with it, savour its meaning before moving on." In so doing you honor the Spirit's prompting, and your own spontaneous prayer happens.[3] Consider memorizing a short phrase (as little as three or four words) from those prayers and carrying it with you through the rest of your day.

At the end of your time, do not rush off. Bask in the silence and refreshment for a few moments.

Orienting Others to the Service Beforehand

At times it may be necessary to orient people to aspects of the service (e.g., version of doxology or Lord's Prayer, where hymns are found, observing silence, how to chant, place of extemporaneous prayers, even practicing a tune). Always do the explaining before the prayers begin and not during them. Lauralee Farrer and Clayton J. Schmit give counsel here that also applies to other worship services: "Try to avoid giving directions throughout each office. . . . Extraneous talk has the power to stifle, even suffocate ritual practices."[4]

After the explanation and orientation, give people time to slow down and collect themselves and prepare to be prayerful. Always proceed at a leisurely pace, and never give the impression of being rushed or in a hurry.

Praying with Scriptures

Remember that the prayers are mostly from the Bible. Office prayer books are a way of using Scriptures to pray, pay attention to God, listen to God, check our lives and bearings alongside Scriptures, interpret our circumstances by Scripture, and ask God to mold our hearts by God's priorities.

I recommend saying or even chanting psalms and canticles aloud. One resource can help with this: Cynthia Bourgeault's *Singing the Psalms: How to Chant in the Christian Contemplative Tradition* (see "Recommended Resources for Morning and Evening Prayer," below). When the texts are oral, not silent, we move more deeply into their meaning. (In earlier centuries, all reading was done out loud.) It is also easier to memorize texts read aloud than ones read silently.

Psalms and canticles often include an antiphon to be said before and after the recitation. This short phrase helps emphasize a certain theme in the text.

Many Christian traditions frequently include the Gloria Patri: "Glory to the Father, and to the Son, and to the Holy Spirit. As it was in the beginning, is now, and will be for ever. Amen." This doxology goes back at least as early as the fourth century and reminds us that our prayers are actually praise.[5] Some Christian communities now pray a different version: "Glory to you, Source of all Being, Eternal Word, and Holy Spirit, as it was in the beginning, is now, and will be forever. Amen."

Read Scriptures slowly and meditatively. During silence you can ask yourself, "Where do I identify with this story or passage?" or "What does God say to me here today?"

After the Scripture readings, pause in silence for at least a few minutes and ponder what God might be saying to you through the texts. Discuss with God what you hear. *Take Our Moments and Our Days* also encourages people who are present to offer brief reflections about the passages of the day, as a way of honoring the Anabaptist conviction that we best learn from the Bible when we interpret it together.

Following the Gospel reading, many prayer books often have a responsory that focuses on a theme from the Scripture.

Choosing Your Scriptures

Make a priority of reading the Bible every day. *Take Our Moments* has short Scripture passages as part of the Call for Discipleship, which are often suitable for memorization. But the hope always was that prayers would be drawn more deeply into the Bible.

It is best to choose a patterned approach and stick with that for a time. Some people read through the Bible *in course*; that is, they start at Genesis, chapter 1, read a chapter a day, and when they come to the last chapter of Revelation, they begin again. Some read one chapter from the Old Testament and one from the New every day. Many Christians pray five psalms a day, thus completing the book every month. Various programs offer outlines for reading through the entire Bible each year. Or you might follow daily lectionaries, which are keyed to the church year.

I find that Bible reading is most fruitful when we are faithful to a pattern and are not choosing each day what we will read and pray.

Intercessions

When praying intercessions, alone or in a group, pause between petitions to name silently or aloud concerns that come to mind. Also give yourself time to incorporate your own prayer list. *Take Our Moments and Our Days* has a deliberate pattern of expanding circles of prayer and invites participants to cite their own particular concerns as well.

It is important to close this time with the Lord's

Prayer, as Christians have done for two millennia. The Lord's Prayer, after all, is the original common prayer for all of us.

Think Like a Choir—Praying in a Group

To get a sense of how to pray this way in a group, consider visiting a monastery, a local church, or another Christian community with such practices. While you may not wish to imitate everything they do, the atmosphere will be instructive, and you may pick up practical tips.

One more pointer: If you are saying prayers in a group, be mindful of the persons praying around you. When singing in a choir, it is important to keep pace with each other and not to outdo each other in volume. I occasionally go to churches where the rule seems to be to sing as loudly as possible. Some of my friends are involved with *Sacred Harp* song-fests, and they tell me that one guideline in that tradition says: "If you can hear your neighbor, then you are not loud enough." Monastic prayer, however, has an opposite emphasis: "If you cannot hear your neighbors, then you are too loud."

If you are fortunate enough to have a group committed to praying common prayer, try to join together at least once a week. Such gatherings not only reinforce and deepen our commitment; they also remind us that our prayers are essentially common or communal. Taizé brothers kept telling me how hard it is to maintain such prayer disciplines without the regular support of others.

Appendix B

Structure and Content of Morning and Evening Prayer

It is good to understand the flow or plot of the Office. Morning and evening prayers evolved and were passed down with a parallel threefold order: praising of God (psalms or hymns), listening to God's Word (usually the day's Gospel reading and other Bible passages), and responding to God's Word (silence, a creed, a hymn or a canticle, and intercessions). The response almost invariably includes the Lord's Prayer, a tradition that goes back to the earliest days of the church. Then the service ends with a blessing.

The following outline is general and may vary somewhat in different Christian traditions. The content may not all be exactly the same, but the order will be similar, and certain key elements will appear in most.

There are various lectionary schemes for knowing which additional Scriptures to read on a given day. Sometimes (as in the *Book of Common Prayer*) the suggestions are in the book itself.

Address God in Praise	Morning Prayer	Evening Prayer
Invitation to Prayer	O Lord, open our lips. And our mouth shall declare your praise.	O God, make speed to save us. O Lord, make haste to help us. Glory to the Father, and to the Son, and to the Holy Spirit. As it was in the beginning, is now, and will be for ever. Amen.
Invitatory Psalm	Psalm 95, 96, 100, 67, 24	
	Hymn	Hymn (possibly with light theme)
	Prayer for Morning	Prayer for Evening
	Psalm: e.g., Psalm 3, 5, 57	Evening Psalm: e.g., Psalm 141, 92, 143, 63, 664, 16
Listen to God	Scripture Lessons	Scripture Lessons
	Old Testament Canticle	New Testament Canticle
	Gospel	Tomorrow's Gospel
	Silence	Silence

Address God in Praise	Morning Prayer	Evening Prayer
Respond to God	Zechariah's Canticle (Benedictus)	Mary's Canticle (Magnificat)
	Intercessions (dedicating day)	Intercessions (for the world's needs)
	Lord's Prayer	Lord's Prayer
	Collect	Collect
	Blessing and Dismissal	Blessing and Dismissal

Appendix C
Preparing a Hospitable Space for Corporate Celebration

When I met with Brother Émile of Taizé, he spoke of the importance of paying attention to preparing and setting up our space for worship and prayer. He talked about the care and deliberation that we give to getting meals ready and making rooms and tables hospitable for entertaining. And then he asked:

> How much care do we take for prayer, the singing, the place? What do we do to make it inviting, warm? The place of prayer says a lot.

I am not visually oriented, but as a pastor I often saw that attention to such details makes a huge difference to many people's engagement in worship. Once my wife and I were looking for a new church and attended a service that impressed both of us greatly. But afterward she surprised me when she said that she could not regularly attend there.

"Why not?" I wondered.

"That sanctuary is too ugly. I'd find it depressing," she responded. In that moment, I saw the importance of paying attention to our worship setting.

Several practical details are worth noting when arranging for corporate prayers:

- Consider using a church building or another place with sacred associations. Praying between prayer-drenched walls not only deepens a sense of reverence; it also is a physical connection with those who have prayed there before and during other times that week.

- Whether or not the room has sacred associations, you can heighten its worshipful quality by placing a simple religious object or two in it: a cross, a Bible, candles, art, or icons. Keep it simple and do not have too many such objects. Cluttered spaces distract and detract from what is central.

- If you are in charge of the service, get there ahead of others. Be sure that chairs are in order, candles are lit, hymnals and prayer books are distributed and neatly arranged by the time others arrive. This way they can settle into a prayerful silence and not be distracted by clutter and busyness.

- Seating can be lined up or curved, facing a focal worship center (a cross, a table) or arranged so that worshippers face each other. What you choose may depend on your theology. Do you want to make a priority of being in community, or should you corporately face away from yourselves and toward a worship point? Monastics pray across from each other. This arrangement also works in Mennonites' congregational theology: The advantage of such a posture is that the sense of community and mutual encouragement is heightened.

- There should be light adequate enough for reading but not too bright. Candles create warm light.
- Have a sufficient number of extra copies of your prayer book available for visitors.
- Make sure that someone pays attention to guests and will orient them by showing how to use the materials and where the prayers are found.

Notes

Foreword

1. Constitution on the Sacred Liturgy, *Sacrosanctum Concilium*, promulgated by Pope Paul VI on December 4, 1963, http://www.vatican.va/archive/hist_councils/ii_vatican_council/documents/vat-ii_const_19631204_sacrosanctum-concilium_en.html.

Acknowledgments

1. Arthur Paul Boers, *The Rhythm of God's Grace: Uncovering Morning and Evening Hours of Prayer* (Brewster, MA: Paraclete Press, 2003).

2. Arthur Paul Boers et al., eds., *Take Our Moments and Our Days: An Anabaptist Prayer Book*, vol. 1, *Ordinary Time*, rev. ed.; vol. 2, *Advent Through Pentecost* (Elkhart, IN: Institute of Mennonite Studies; Scottdale, PA: Herald Press, 2010); http://www.ambs.edu/news-and-publications/prayerbook/content.

3. *Praise in All Our Days: Common Prayer at Taizé; Liturgies for the Entire Year in Modern English*, rev. ed., trans. of *La louange des jours* (London: Mowbray, 1981).

Introduction

1. See note 1 for Acknowledgments.
2. See note 2 for Acknowledgments.

Chapter 1: Finding a Lost Treasure

1. See note 3 for Acknowledgments.

2. Douglas V. Steere, *Together in Solitude* (New York: Crossroad, 1982), 25.

3. C. W. McPherson, *Grace at This Time: Praying the Daily Office* (Harrisburg, PA: Morehouse, 1999), 1.

4. These translations are from The Episcopal Church's *Book of Common Prayer* (New York: Seabury, 1979), 115–16.

5. Phyllis Tickle, compiler, *The Divine Hours*, 3 vols., *Prayers for Summertime*, *Prayers for Autumn and Wintertime*, and *Prayers for Springtime* (New York: Doubleday, 2000–2001); idem, *The Shaping of a Life: A Spiritual Landscape* (New York: Doubleday, 2001).

6. Frances R. Havergal, "Take My Life," in *Hymnal: A Worship Book* (Scottdale, PA: Herald Press, 1992), no. 389, adapted.

Chapter 2: The Common Prayer of Uncommon Communities

1. Andy Raine and John T. Skinner, compilers, *Celtic Daily Prayer: From the Northumbria Community*, rev. and updated ed. (London: HarperCollins, 2000; first ed., London: MarshallPickering, 1994).

2. Arthur Paul Boers, *The Way Is Made by Walking: A Pilgrimage along the Camino de Santiago* (Downers Grove, IL: InterVarsity Press, 2007).

Chapter 3: Ancient Rhythms of Prayer

1. David Mitchell, *The Thousand Autumns of Jacob de Zoet* (Toronto: Knopf Canada; New York: Random House, 2010).

2. Steere, *Together in Solitude*, 25.

3. Suzanne Guthrie, *Praying the Hours* (Cambridge, MA: Cowley, 2000), 67.

4. D. H. Farmer, ed., "The Voyage of St. Brendan," in *The Age of Bede*, trans. J. F. Webb (New York: Penguin Books, 1998), 243.

5. Maya Angelou, *I Know Why the Caged Bird Sings* (New York: Ballantine Books, 1991), 5.

6. Chalmer E. Faw, *Acts*, Believers Church Bible Commentary (Scottdale, PA: 1993), 48.

7. Arthur Paul Boers, *Lord, Teach Us to Pray: A New Look at the Lord's Prayer* (Scottdale, PA: Herald Press, 1992).

8. Joachim Jeremias, *The Prayers of Jesus*, trans. John Bowden et al. (Philadelphia: Fortress, 1967), 77–78.

9. Massey H. Shepherd, Jr., *The Paschal Liturgy and the Apocalypse* (Richmond, VA: John Knox Press, 1960), 73.

10. John Brook, *The School of Prayer: An Introduction to the Divine Office for All Christians* (Collegeville, MN: Liturgical Press, 1992), 9.

Chapter 4: Where Have All the Hours Gone?

1. Paul Bradshaw, *Two Ways of Praying* (Nashville: Abingdon, 1995), 17–21. We do not look at all of his contrasts here.

2. Roger S. Wieck, *Time Sanctified: The Book of Hours in Medieval Art and Life* (New York: George Braziller, 1988), 27.

3. Information and quotes in these two paragraphs are from J. Neil Alexander, "Luther's Reform of the Daily Office," *Worship* 57, no. 4 (July 1983): 349–51, 359.

4. Paul Bradshaw, "Whatever Happened to Daily Prayer?" *Worship* 64, no. 1 (January 1990): 19. Eamon Duffy suggests that the English Reformation greatly harmed the personal prayer practices of many laypersons: "When all is said and done, the Reformation was a violent disruption, not the natural fulfillment, of most of what was vigorous in late medieval piety and religious practice." *The Stripping of the Altars: Traditional Religion in England, c. 1400–c. 1580* (New Haven: Yale University Press, 1992), 4.

5. Quotes and ideas in this paragraph are from Bradshaw, *Two Ways of Praying*, 36, 40–41.

6. John Rempel, ed., *Minister's Manual* (Scottdale, PA: Herald Press, 1998), 15.

7. John H. Yoder, trans. and ed., *The Legacy of Michael Sattler* (Scottdale, PA: Herald Press, 1973), 44, 54n105.

8. James Wm. McClendon Jr., "Balthasar Hubmaier, Catholic Anabaptist," in *Essays in Anabaptist Theology*, ed. H. Wayne Pipkin (Elkhart, IN: Institute of Mennonite Studies, 1974), 73. See also Torsten Bergsten, *Balthasar Hubmaier: Anabaptist Theologian and Martyr*, trans. W. R. Estep Jr. (Valley Forge, PA: Judson, 1978), 325, 545n24.

9. Marion Kobelt-Groch, "Why Did Petronella Leave Her Husband? Reflections on Marital Avoidance among the Halberstadt Anabaptists," *Mennonite Quarterly Review* 62, no. 1 (January 1988): 27.

10. Claus-Peter Clasen, *Anabaptism: A Social History, 1525–1618* (Ithaca, NY: Cornell University Press, 1972), 276.

11. Information in this paragraph is derived from Harold S. Bender, "Prayer Books, Mennonite," in *The Mennonite Encyclopedia*, vol. 4 (Scottdale, PA: Mennonite Publishing House, 1959), 211; the most detailed summary and analysis of Mennonite prayer books is found in Robert Friedmann's, *Mennonite Piety through the Centuries* (Scottdale, PA: Mennonite Publishing House, 1949).

12. Friedmann considers this one of the most important prayer books and notes that portions of it are plagiarized from a 1539 prayer book by Caspar Schwenckfeld. Friedmann calls *Ernsthafte* "the first completely furnished and self-contained German prayer book for Mennonites." Friedmann, *Mennonite Piety*, 189–195.

13. Leonard Gross, trans., *Prayer Book for Earnest Christians* (Scottdale, PA: Herald Press, 1997); Elizabeth Bender and Leonard Gross, trans., *Golden Apples in Silver Bowls* (Lancaster: Lancaster Mennonite Historical Society, 1999).

14. *A Devoted Christian's Prayer Book* (LaGrange, IN: Pathway Publishers, 2003).

15. Information about the Nickel Mines Amish comes from conversations and correspondence

with Donald B. Kraybill and Steven M. Nolt and quotes are from the book they coauthored with David L. Weaver-Zercher, *Amish Grace: How Forgiveness Transcended Tragedy* (San Francisco: Jossey-Bass, 2007), 90–98. The businessman's quote is from that book.

Chapter 5: Day by Day These Things We Pray

1. Dorotheos of Gaza, *Discourses and Sayings: Desert Humor and Humility*, trans. Eric P. Wheeler (Kalamazoo, MI: Cistercian Publications, 1977), 176–77.

2. Timothy Fry et al., eds., *RB 1980: The Rule of St. Benedict in Latin and English with Notes* (Collegeville, MN: Liturgical Press, 1981), 47; cf. idem, *The Rule of St. Benedict in English* (New York: Vintage Books, 1998).

3. Clyde Edgerton, *Walking across Egypt* (New York: Ballantine Books, 1987), 82.

4. As quoted in Wendy M. Wright, *The Time Between: Cycles and Rhythms in Ordinary Time* (Nashville: Upper Room, 2000), 30.

5. John Cassian, *The Conferences*, trans. Boniface Ramsey (New York: Paulist Press, 1997), 739–40.

6. Eugene H. Peterson, *Working the Angles: The Shape of Pastoral Integrity* (Grand Rapids: Eerdmans, 1987), 48.

7. Izaak Walton, as quoted by John N. Wall Jr., "Introduction," in George Herbert's *The Country Parson; The Temple*, ed. John N. Wall Jr. (Mahwah, NJ: Paulist Press, 1981), 7.

8. Brother Abraham, "Monk's Best Friend," *Abbey Letter* (of St. Gregory's Abbey), no. 242 (Summer 2010): 1.

9. Dorothy C. Bass, *Receiving the Day: Christian Practices for Opening the Gift of Time* (San Francisco: Jossey-Bass, 2000), 12.

10. Heather Murray Elkins, cited from Donna Schaper, *Sabbath Keeping* (Cambridge, MA: Cowley, 1999), 9–10.

11. George Guiver, *Company of Voices: Daily Prayer and the People of God* (New York: Pueblo, 1988), 15.

12. As cited in Brook, *School of Prayer*, 5–6.

13. Charles Cummings, *Monastic Practices* (Kalamazoo, MI: Cistercian Publications, 1986), 78–79.

Chapter 6: The Freedom of Disciplines

1. "Equal Time for Norwegian Atheists," *Christian Century* 117, no. 13 (April 19–26, 2000): 453–54.

2. Read this astonishing story in John W. Kiser, *The Monks of Tibhirine: Faith, Love, and Terror in Algeria* (New York: St. Martin's Press, 2002).

3. William Dalrymple, *From the Holy Mountain: A Journey in the Shadow of Byzantium* (London: HarperCollins, 1998), 168.

4. Fry, *RB 1980*, 215, 217.

5. Clement is cited in James Houston, *The Transforming Friendship: A Guide to Prayer* (Batavia, IL: Lion Publishing, 1989), 6.

6. Elizabeth Barrett Browning, *Aurora Leigh* (1857), book 7, http://digital.library.upenn.edu/women/barrett/aurora/aurora.html#7.

7. These traditional monastic prayers are found in the prayer booklet of St. Gregory's Abbey, *Divine Office at Saint Gregory's Abbey* (Three Rivers, MI: Self published, no date).

8. Cited in a "Reflections" column, *Christianity Today*, October 22, 1990, 43.

9. Benedicta Ward, trans., *The Sayings of the Desert Fathers* (Kalamazoo, MI: Cistercian Publications, 1975), 3–4.

Chapter 7: Wrestling for a Blessing

1. Robert Ellsberg, *All Saints: Daily Reflections on Saints, Prophets, and Witnesses for Our Time* (New York: Crossroad, 1997), 261.

2. Dietrich Bonhoeffer, *Life Together*, trans. John W. Doberstein (New York: Harper & Row, 1954), 64.

3. Quotes and ideas in this paragraph are from William H. Willimon and Stanley Hauerwas, *Lord, Teach Us: The Lord's Prayer and the Christian Life* (Nashville: Abingdon, 1996), 16–20.

4. Joan Chittister, *Wisdom Distilled from the Daily: Living the Rule of St. Benedict Today* (San Francisco: Harper, 1991), 31.

5. Yushi Nomura, *Desert Wisdom: Sayings from the Desert Fathers* (New York: Doubleday, 1982), 59.

6. As quoted by Debra K. Farrington, *Living Faith Day by Day* (New York: Perigee, 2000), 81.

7. McPherson, *Grace at This Time*, 87.

Chapter 8: Giving at the Office

1. Richard J. Foster, *Prayer: Finding the Heart's True Home* (San Francisco: HarperCollins, 1992), 106.

2. Ibid., 107–8.

3. Mark Galli, "Memorable Speech," *Christianity Today*, January 8, 2001, 9.

4. Brook, *School of Prayer*, 3–4.

5. Lisa Belcher Hamilton, *For Those We Love but See No Longer: Daily Offices for Times of Grief* (Brewster, MA: Paraclete Press, 2001), xv.

6. Eugene H. Peterson, *Under the Unpredictable Plant: An Exploration in Vocational Holiness* (Grand Rapids: Eerdmans, 1992), 101.

7. Ibid., 102–3.

8. Brook, *School of Prayer*, 89.

9. Esther Quinlan, "Sailing Home," *Sacred Journey* 52, no. 4 (August 2001): 33, 37.

10. Kerry Kelly, "Laying the Cornerstone for Christian Unity," *Catholic New Times*, June 11, 2000, 12.

11. Phyllis Tickle, "What Drew Me In and Kept Me Practicing Fixed Hour Prayer," http://www.explorefaith.org/prayer/fixed/tickle.html. Downloaded August 9, 2010.

Chapter 9: Testing the Waters

1. John H. Westerhoff III and William H. Willimon, *Liturgy and Learning through the Life Cycle* (Akron, OH: OSL [Order of Saint Luke] Publications, 1994), 81.

2. *The Grail Psalms: Translated from the Hebrew—Singing Version; Arranged to the Psalmody of Joseph Gelineau* (London: Collins, 1963, plus reprints).

Epilogue
1. For *The Grail Psalms*, see note 2 for chapter 9.

Appendix A
1. Don Postema, *Space for God: The Study and Practice of Prayer and Spirituality* (Grand Rapids: Bible Way, 1983), 17.

2. McPherson, *Grace at This Time*, 90.

3. Brook, *School of Prayer*, 29.

4. Farrer and Schmit, *Praying the Hours*, 25.

5. McPherson, *Grace at This Time*, 28.

Recommended Resources for Morning and Evening Prayer

Benson, Robert. *In Constant Prayer*. Nashville: Thomas Nelson, 2008. A lyrical and evocative writer who imaginatively shares with us his own testimony of the blessings of entering into common prayer traditions.

Boers, Arthur Paul, et al, eds. *Take Our Moments and Our Days: An Anabaptist Prayer Book*, vol. 1, *Ordinary Time*, rev. ed.; vol. 2, *Advent Through Pentecost* (Elkhart, IN: Institute of Mennonite Studies; Scottdale, PA: Herald Press, 2010). These prayer books fulfill the priorities that have been explored in this volume. As described in the Epilogue, they were developed in wide consultation with church folk throughout North America and around the world. Their words are adapted primarily from the Bible with a particular focus on the life, words, and teachings of Jesus. Language is used carefully and lovingly, and singing is encouraged.

Bourgeault, Cynthia. *Singing the Psalms: How to Chant in the Christian Contemplative Tradition*. Boulder, CO: Sounds True, 1997. This charming, occasionally quirky, and informative package of recordings teaches both how and why to chant the Psalms. It contains a wealth of information about common prayer and even about *lectio divina*, an ancient method of engaging Scriptures prayerfully.

Bradshaw, Paul F. *Two Ways of Praying*. Nashville: Abingdon, 1995. A leading worship scholar shows how church worship and private prayer became disconnected. He argues for reconnecting the two by reinvigorating common prayer.

Brook, John. *The School of Prayer: An Introduction to the Divine Office for All Christians*. Collegeville, MN: Liturgical Press, 1992. A useful handbook for the liturgy of the hours: its theology, contents, and purposes.

Farrer, Lauralee, and Clayton J. Schmit. *Praying the Hours: In Ordinary Life* (Eugene OR: Cascade Books, 2010). Written by Protestants who are recent converts to the joys of the daily office. It includes rationales, history, and theology, as well as eight services for throughout the day. It is beautifully written, with occasional glimpses of humor too: "The closest thing to ancient tradition in my church was anything made with lime Jell-O," writes Ms. Farrer.

Guiver, George. *Company of Voices: Daily Prayer and the People of God*. New York: Pueblo, 1988. One of my favorite books on the history and theology of the Office, with lots of information and insights.

Guthrie, Suzanne. *Praying the Hours*. Cambridge, MA: Cowley, 2000. This short, pleasantly written volume reflects on the value of common prayer.

McPherson, C. W. *Grace at This Time: Praying the Daily Office*. Harrisburg, PA: Morehouse, 1999.

Written by an American Episcopal priest, this is the best and easiest-to-read introduction to common prayer that I have found. Highly recommended.

Taft, Robert. *The Liturgy of the Hours in East and West: The Origins of the Divine Office and Its Meaning for Today.* Collegeville, MN: Liturgical Press, 1986. If you want history and scholarship, this is the classic and indispensable text on understanding Christian traditions of common prayer.

The Author

Arthur Boers holds the R. J. Bernardo Family Chair of Leadership at Tyndale Seminary (Toronto, Canada). He previously taught pastoral theology at Associated Mennonite Biblical Seminary (Elkhart, Indiana).

A Benedictine oblate, Arthur served for more than sixteen years as a pastor in rural, urban, and church-planting settings in the United States and Canada.

He has written six books in all, including *The Way is Made by Walking: A Pilgrimage Along the Camino de Santiago* (InterVarsity, 2007) reflecting on an 800-kilometer / 497-mile pilgrimage that he walked in Spain and *Never Call Them Jerks: Healthy Responses to Difficult Behavior* (Alban, 1999).